ADVANC
DYIN

"My wife and I have known Pastor Marvin for many years, and I know how his spiritual journey to serve Jesus Christ has had its share of tribulations and blessings. I have witnessed his tireless work to minister to those the world has forgotten and tossed aside, but who Christ and the church have called him to bring home. His passion is exciting and contagious. His grace and compassion truly witnesses to the transforming power of Jesus Christ! The book and ministry is "now" for a world to read and experience Christ's redeeming power of forgiveness, grace, and mercy! This book is a must-read for persons, churches, and families impacted as a result of crime and the criminal justice system. Praise Jesus Christ for Pastor Marvin and his willingness to openly share the transforming power of the gospel of Jesus Christ revealed in his life!"

—Larry Miller

"This is a man after God's own heart: teaching, preaching, coaching, mentoring, facilitating in many venues, and encouraging life-changing transformations, both spiritual and social."

—Claudette Busby Singletary

"I have known Pastor Marvin for nearly thirty-five years, having watched him grow up in prison where he graduated college and grew exponentially in his spiritual life. His testimony, passion, and compassion to share the gospel of Jesus Christ with others who have been impacted by crime and incarceration is a testament to the transforming power of Jesus Christ. This is a true story and a must-read for all people who have a genuine interest in the criminal justice system and in God's saving grace."

—Mickey Liles, Retired Warden,
Texas Department of Criminal Justice

"We have known Pastor Marvin for over twenty-five years. We have witnessed how Jesus Christ transformed his life after prison and how his tireless work in ministry has carried the gospel of Jesus Christ to incarcerated offenders and throughout the faith community. His story is truly a testament to the transforming power of Jesus Christ and a must-read for anyone impacted by crime, including families, victims, prison ministries, and those interested in criminal justice or criminal justice reform."

—Jim Willett, Retired Warden, Texas Department of Criminal Justice, and Janice Willett, Retired Director of Institutional Parole Operations, Texas Board of Pardons and Paroles

"Having met Pastor Marvin twenty years ago, I realized, then till now, how profound and unique he teaches the word of God. As a member of his church, I have been greatly blessed by his ministry, teaching, and friendship."

—Kenneth Hunter, Information Technology (IT), G6 Deployment Project Manager

DYING TO LIVE

DYING TO LIVE

A Miraculous Restoration

MARVIN W. HOOD

DYING TO LIVE

Published by Purposely Created Publishing Group™

Printed in the United States of America

ISBN: 978-1-64484-142-6

DEDICATION

This book is dedicated to my loving wife, Bonita. Thank you for your loving support, confidence, and trust. It is also dedicated to my mother, Juanita Hood, who told me she had me to preach for God. Mother, I am doing what God and you told me to do.

This is a true story that could not have been written without the power and guidance of the Holy Spirit in Jesus Christ. This story was an idea that I held inside for many years before expressing it in writing. I thought I did not have the skills or the patience to start such a project, much less complete it. This is not just another story about a man in prison being saved. The story is about how the power of God through Jesus Christ has worked in my life, for all my life, beginning as a three-year-old infant in my mother's lap. I realized that I did not have the proper writing training required for this type of endeavor, so I procrastinated. Because of the power of the Holy Spirit of God, however, I became more afraid of not writing about something that would honor God in Christ than of writing. I am a man who has learned to fear God with great reverence, so when he said I needed to write the story, I began to write.

This story began as a sermon response about social issues, but the power of the Holy Spirit took control over me, providing the insight, strength, and guidance to begin the work and bring it to completion. My fear of God was both my reverence to him and the obedience in me to persevere until it was completed. I wrote every day under the unction and power of the Holy Spirit—I wrote for weeks, day and night, with an insatiable urge to fulfill this task before either the guidance of the Holy Spirit would leave me or I would lose my patience. This book depicts my spiritual journey and life, through which I began to see the evidence that Christ was always at the helm in my life. This is Christ's story, and it was his will that compelled me to share it, to express and reveal his great transforming power. I knew I was not a writer, but when the time came to write this story, the Holy Spirit compelled me that it was time to "write it down," just as God gave the same order to the prophet Habakkuk (Habakkuk 2:2).

CONTENTS

ACKNOWLEDGMENTS

Special thanks to my wife, Bonita. Thank you for your love, patience, encouragement, and resolve in the presence of scorn, insults, and ridicule, and for choosing to build a life with someone who has a past.

Thanks to those in the Texas Annual Conference of the United Methodist for their acceptance, support, and nurture.

Thanks to everyone on my core team for your commitment to the Lord and your committed service to our church and congregation, especially Mark Brooker, David & Sabie Tisdel, Jack & Francine Doyle, Marshall & Denise Schoth, Ken Hunter, Charlesetta Busby, Bridgette Busby, Larry & Rachael Miller, Latoya & Mike Figgs, and Claudette & Jimmy Singletary.

Thanks to my editor, Dr. Kevin Hrebik, for stretching me to write more, to dig deeper into the past bedrock of my pain where I suffered, but more importantly to articulate the place where I died in Jesus Christ to live again.

Thanks to all who supported me among friends, chaplains, wardens, and others retired from the Texas Department of Criminal Justice, who knew me and watched me grow up in prison, but who cared for me as a person when it was considered not in good taste to care for an inmate. Some of their testimonies are in the back of the book.

Space does not permit naming everyone to whom I am grateful, but please know that you are indelibly etched on my mind and heart.

PREFACE

In January 1977 I was arrested for unauthorized use of a motor vehicle, but due to a newly passed law and an ambitious district attorney who wanted to make use of it, I was indicted for aggravated robbery with a deadly weapon. I was told to plead guilty for a sentence of fifteen years, but I refused because I was not guilty of the indicted offense. I tried to convey to the court that I was arrested for unauthorized use of a motor vehicle, but the court's response was uncaring. All they wanted to hear was a guilty plea, or I would be thrown away. I was twenty-two years old and I thought my life was over.

> But he was wounded for our transgressions, crushed for our iniquities; upon him was the punishment that made us whole, and by his bruises we are healed. All we like sheep have gone astray; we have all turned to our own way, and the Lord has laid on him the iniquity of us all. He was oppressed, and he was afflicted, yet he did not open his mouth; like a lamb that is led to the slaughter, and like a sheep that before its shearers is silent, so he did not open his mouth. By a perversion of justice he was taken away. Who could have imagined his future? For he was cut off from the land of the living, stricken for the transgression of my people.
>
> —Isaiah 53:5–8

This book did not start with the intention to write a personal story about my life. Rather, it started as a spiritual response, to speak to the critical problems and broken policies regarding criminal justice issues, law enforcement, and general distrust of the policing community. I have personal experiences with these entities as a former prisoner, and then years later as a pastor of a restorative justice ministry. As I witnessed the current crises troubling the state of law and order institutions and of society in general today, I became deeply saddened to see some of the same judicial injustices, legal mistreatment of black Americans, and police distrust that were prevalent fifty years ago. I am a preacher, however, so I understand things through scripture, and that perspective comprises the heart of my response to these issues.

My hurt and sadness are not merely in response to that which the news media is reporting; rather, they are about historical truths that have never died or healed. What we are currently seeing are resurgences of the past in search of healing. People may forget the past, but the past will not forget its truth. These are realities that will not simply fade away, and unfortunately some of these realities are still alive and well, still seeking a way to be heard. Truth has a need to be free, too. This reality should be evident because some of the same social issues of racism and racial discrepancies that were pervasive in the first century of the nation are still present today. Healing was never meant to be harmful, although it is usually messy and painful.

Silence has something to say, but it needs a catalyst to convey its message. The only catalyst for getting the message out to the masses is through the voices of God's ministers and people. God usually sends people to proclaim himself.

Since some of the people who have the resources to get the message out have not honestly told the truths that must be spoken, the truth will seek alternate venues to express itself. Perhaps it may be difficult to recognize, but there is a reason the truth will stand to tell its truth when it has been too long suffocated, repressed, exploited, manipulated, and boldly lied about. This has been done to cover shameful depravities of unwholesome truths and dishonorable vestiges considered socially outdated, and it is vehemently denied that these cruel realities continue to exist today. "Jesus said to [Thomas], 'I am the way, and the truth, and the life'" (John 14:6a). Lies are dead things, and they require more lies to perpetuate the existing dead lies. When the truth cannot rely on people to speak truth, the Father sent the truth into the world to testify of itself. When men refuse to tell the truth, the truth will stand up and speak of itself. "He who is in [me] is greater than he who is in the world" (1 John 4:4b).

The root of the issue is not just criminals who are breaking the law and perpetuating senseless violence. Rather, the violence, law breaking, and social unrest are responses to unjust police beatings and killings. These exacerbate and crack open unhealed wounds of the past and present treatment of black men in particular, caused by systemic judicial inequality and punishment. The current responses are inseparably connected to unresolved past injustices, and present logistics that are masked by legislation and institutionalized racial bigotry. It is all right to be angry about social injustices regarding any governing authority of justice and law, but what is not honorable or justifiable is the unwillingness to honestly, genuinely address the real issues with truth and authenticity.

The current crisis will not be silently washed away, nor will it fade away on its own, because the issues are about people. The issues cannot be resolved without a spiritual reorientation of mind, knowledge, and reality (Romans 12:2).

INTRODUCTION

> No words can express how much the world owes to sorrow. Most of the Psalms were born in a wilderness. Most of the Epistles were written in a prison. The greatest thoughts of the greatest thinkers have all passed through fire. The greatest poets have "learned in suffering what they thought in song." In bonds, Bunyan lived the allegory that he afterward indicted, and we may thank Bedford Jail for the *Pilgrim's Progress*. "Take comfort, afflicted Christian! When God is about to make preeminent use of a man, He puts him in the fire."[1]
>
> —George MacDonald

This story of transformation is about the power of God and the blood of Jesus Christ. As stated previously, even though I knew I was not a writer, I ventured into the project out of simple obedience. As I started writing, however, I began to be compelled by my compassion about the current crisis that America is facing. As I began to express my sentiments, I started to realize at the same time the depth of the current crisis. I realized that what is happening in America—between law enforcement, the criminal justice system, and the disconnect and loss of trust between the policing community and mass communities at large—is

1. AZ Quotes, "George MacDonald Quotes," accessed Dec. 24, 2017, http://www.azquotes.com/author/9199-George_MacDonald.

deeply rooted in the disease of racism. Racism should be considered a disease because its nature is illusive and secretive; it knows how to hide, and it is manipulative, vague, obstinate, obtrusive, and viciously ugly.

Because of its nature, racism requires a power beyond men to change its nature and obliterate the substance from the deepest roots. The system of criminal justice, including law enforcement, judicial entities, and the police community, are on one side of the issue—and the torn ligaments of distrust toward the criminal justice system, comprised of all the elements above, are on the other. What neither side can see is that the justice system will never reconcile with the people of color in our nation until America repents to God in Jesus Christ and confesses its sins, including both its open and hidden sins. The problems will not dissipate until America confesses, not with their mouths but with their hearts. The heart is what God sees, and he will not be mocked. Only God has the power to transform America and honorably sanitize the American conscience. Only God has the answers for the disease and plague of racism. No other solution—not even another Civil War—will resolve this pernicious issue, which is as deep and evil as sin itself in the human heart.

This story began as an outpouring of my experiences with the dark side of the justice system, but quickly became a reflection of the bigger reality in my life—the story of my redemption and transformation, engineered and conducted by God in his power and love. What was true for me—that I needed a major wakeup call to turn back to God—is true on a bigger scale for the nation. Until the American people restore their conscience of godly presence and godly obedience back into their institutions and emulate the practices and character of Jesus Christ, as required by God, the nation will continue to deteriorate and self-destruct, because too many among us refuse to recognize that the world and all its creation belong to God and God alone.

This story is dedicated to God in Jesus Christ in all his power and glory. The scriptures warned us about what God said about himself—he told us that he was a jealous God. "God is not man, that he should lie, or a son of man, that he should repent" (Numbers 23:19a). America should reconsider just who God is if she wants to be healed. She needs to reacquire a healthy fear of God before her present path of stubborn resistance to him results in irreversible self-destruction from inner corruption—no different than the epic failure of the Roman Empire.

I wrestled within myself about writing this book. I realize that there are many men and women marked and branded for life by the criminal justice system in America. I thought, what difference would my story make among countless others who are condemned, who are invisible and considered subhuman, outcast, unworthy of the same liberties and freedoms others enjoy? And all this even though they have paid their punishment debts with incarceration and demonstrated remorse and personal rehabilitation, psychologically and socially. But they continue to wear the dirty label of felon.

However, I also realized that there are many men and women who may not have the availability and resources to share their story, or who may feel compelled to remain in the shadows or on the sidelines in life. These people may feel coerced out of their God-given blessings to live free and actively participate in the great blessing of life, to live unafraid, unabashed, and with an un-denied access to life. Although each story is different, the people they are about may feel pushed out of society and treated like the lepers spoken of in the Holy Bible in Luke 17:11–19.

I was compelled by the power of the Holy Spirit and by the living Savior Jesus Christ to come out of the shadows of shame, which I realized only held me hostage. But more than myself, the shame would impede the transforming power of Jesus Christ in my life, and remove not just another story of injustice from the world, but also an opportunity for the glory of Jesus Christ to show his justice in an unjust society. It is not my intention to bring glory to myself; instead, it is my honor as a guest of the Holy Spirit to reveal the light and glory of Jesus Christ in my life, and to reveal it to others who may feel invisible or afraid while crying out their desire to live freely in honor, integrity, and social decency.

There are those, in law enforcement and as personal citizens, who have made unwise choices that caused harm and hurt toward others, choices that may or may not have been malicious, just as there are those who have made unwise decisions not from a criminal cause with malicious intent, but rather out of personal, social, or psychological dynamics, mostly out of aberrant behavior such as chemical addiction, toxic family dynamics, or personal hurt and abandonment. It is not my intention to disparage the criminal justice system, the custodians of the courts, or law enforcement. Instead, I commend those who uphold their oath to serve and protect all people with honor, truth, and unbiased commitment.

My hope is that this story may encourage those who feel counted out as irrelevant, who feel like no one of significance, to stand and speak their story, even when it hurts and recants the brokenness of past experiences. I hope this story may inspire other persons, brothers or sisters, fathers, mothers, grandmothers, or loved ones, to speak out against criminal injustice or any injustice that hurts or denigrates anyone, even when the perpetrator may be at fault. The fault should not remove the perpetrator's humanity or their right to treatment as a person.

I hope those who read my story who are genuinely interested in understanding and are concerned enough may become progressively encouraged to move forward toward implementing a more justice-oriented criminal justice system, one reformed to be less punitive and retributive. Those who may have been offended or hurt as a result of criminal misconduct, I share with you my condolences, pray for your healing, and ask for your forgiveness for those who may have hurt you and for those whom I, too, have caused hurt, as well as for those who have caused me hurt.

I hope my story will speak to the larger society of those who have been affected or hurt by the criminal justice system—victims of crime, families impacted as a result of crime and incarceration, ministries, offenders, and criminal justice professionals—to remind us that society is a paradigm of people, race, and class, ethnic, and cultural differences, but we all share the same world and one God.

We live in a society of social stratification, where class, power, prestige, culture, ethnicity, and wealth often influence our social institutions, but we can still remember that it was our Lord God who first gave us all life, and it was God who was the first to show us the way toward forgiveness.

May this book become an inspiration and encouragement for all who may read it. May the light and compassion of Jesus Christ's redeeming grace and transforming power become present to those who read this story. I harbor no hostility or resentment toward anyone, for the events of what happened to me are more the story of Jesus Christ than it is mine. Praise Jesus Christ for his redeeming power and reconciling grace! Love and peace to all!

In Christ,
Pastor Marvin W. Hood, Founding Pastor
Newgate Fellowship United Methodist Church

CHAPTER I

RESURGENCE—HOW FAR MUST YESTERDAY GO TO BECOME PRESENT?

> For every century there is a crisis in our democracy, the response to which defines how future generations view those who were alive at the time. In the eighteenth century it was the transatlantic slave trade, in the nineteenth century it was slavery, in the twentieth century it was Jim Crow. Today it is mass incarceration.[2]
>
> —Benjamin Todd Jealous, President and CEO, NAACP

Several widely-televised instances of social violence in recent years have moved me to respond to the current racial crisis within our society. I am disturbed about the recent disruptions revealing the disconnect between policing and community. Although I am disturbed, I am neither naïve about nor surprised by these disruptions. On one hand, I know and recognize with great respect the need for law enforcement—I sincerely respect law enforcement's authority and I respect officers as persons. On the other hand, I also recognize that some abusive authority and apathy exists in law enforcement's response toward African Americans.

2. Michelle Alexander, *The New Jim Crow in the Age of Colorblindness* (New York: The New Press, 2012), back cover.

As a community, we must encourage a stronger relationship between the two worlds, with more transparency and better communication between law enforcement and the communities they serve. Destructive responses are harmful to both entities because we both live in the same world, and destruction does not have an address. But while we share the same world, we have a stratified society. What we have seen recently between policing and the communities is not new to the black community. It has only become more exposed via social media, and then it becomes news, but it is certainly not new news—it is only nationally reported news because of increased media exposure and the instant awareness made possible by technology.

The violence on both sides (police and communities) has recently escalated, but the collective consensus of police attitudes toward blacks has been a quiet storm that has been resident within the criminal justice system for a very long time. It becomes more visible when the violence of shooting a black person (usually men) occurs, but this type of fire has been smoldering perpetually for generations. The cry and need for change within the criminal justice system, especially among police, has been screaming for decade after decade, but it appears to only get attention after highly publicized killings. Each death digs a deeper grave for us as a society. When funeral processions fill the streets with mourners heading to the cemetery, they carry more than bodies senselessly taken; they carry a sense of our collective social wellbeing.

Try to imagine life for a minute from the perspective of the average black person who has a criminal record:

You may decide not to say anything about it because you think it may start a fight, so you stay quiet about it and say nothing. Then you begin to process food costs, work transportation (bus tokens or paying a person to take you to work), personal hygiene, clothes, washing/cleaners, haircuts, and trying to look good. You don't spend much, just enough so that you are comfortable, but there is not enough money to adequately live on, only to survive. You want to live, not merely survive, and you begin to process your options again, maybe writing all your expenses down so you can see and realize how much you need to have a life. And, bam! You think to yourself, I will never get ahead or ever have anything in life, making this kind of change. I need to do something where I can start making some cheese instead of chump change.

You scroll your phone, looking for the right number that can hook you up. You make the connection and everything is already waiting for you; all you need to do is get there. Hanging up the phone, you tell the person on the other end, hold tight baby, I'm on my way. As you prepare to go wherever you are going, you begin to think about all the difficult challenges facing you and how unpaid you are on anybody's job. You begin to assess your worth and your abilities. Your priorities were in the right place, but you were not in the right place to pull down the type of living you had in mind . . . before getting out of prison.

A couple of years go by, and you may say to yourself, all that's over, because I tried, I really tried, but trying to do it the right way just hasn't been working for me. As you are discussing ways to justify your decisions, your conscience begins to have a conversation with you about the decision you are in process of making, and how it's not too late to turn around. This happens while you are riding the bus to your location, or maybe when someone is driving you there. You arrive at your destination, and your hookup is staring you in the face with all the help . . . and all the misery you need. But you are a man of your word, so you step into someone else's world, even knowing that the minute you face up, you know you are face down, because the hookup is looking down on you as someone with no power and no money. You can feel being looked down on, you know it is present, but all you have is your word, and you can't go out like that. So you think . . . and you think hard . . . what if, just this once, you crossed your own conscience, just because you're so tired of feeling so low for so long?

The longer and more frequent the funeral processions are, the wider and deeper the collective societal grave. The more killings we suffer, the greater the sickness of our shared social health. With each new event, our already polarized society becomes even more divided and mean-spirited toward each other. Is it any wonder that this pattern simultaneously dilutes morals and escalates violence on both sides?

A Systemic Issue; An American Issue

> Where Justice is denied, where poverty is enforced, where ignorance prevails, and where any one class is made to feel that society is an organized conspiracy to oppress, rob and degrade them, neither person nor property will be safe.[3]
>
> —Frederick Douglass

The perception and behavior of law enforcement toward black Americans has continued to be apathetically perpetuated for decades, before and after the reformation of the 1960s. The perception has become institutionally systemic, and the behavior appears to have become socially tolerated, accepted, and resurgent. Of course, not all police/law enforcement share the same behavior, and it is imperative not to stereotype or perceive all law enforcement as having the same mentality. The virtues of moral character and human decency are both good and bad among all people. All members of any group are not the same just because they belong to or work within any given entity. Even when that entity has an appearance of social prejudices and racial divisiveness, it is often insidiously propagated by a relatively low percentage of small

3. From a speech on the twenty-fourth anniversary of emancipation in the District of Columbia, Washington, D.C., Apr. 1886. AZ Quotes, "Frederick Douglass Quotes," accessed Dec. 24, 2017, http://www.azquotes.com/author/4104-Frederick_Douglass.

and narrow minds within their ranks. The problem is that major diseases start as small infections.

The Apostle Paul wrote about how to manage people with this type of mentality by "heaping burning coals on their heads" (Romans 12:20). This Bible verse is not meant to convey any sense of hurt or revenge, but quite the opposite, in that responding with kindness to one's enemies is meant to encourage and reveal a better person inside each of us—inside both parties. This biblical response is especially applicable toward someone who has subscribed to any racial rhetoric that incites, instigates, or propagates racial biases and divisiveness. This type of behavior could be a signal about some character issues that may need personal examination. Change often comes solely through revelation that comes from within, but it also can be initiated by the hot coals of shame created by kindness in response to ugliness.

Personal discoveries like this can become stressful, however, because they often compel us to stretch ourselves beyond our normal, personal spaces and character. Personal change most often is resistant and untidy. I once read a book by Ralph M. Lewis entitled *The Conscious Interlude*, and I gathered from it that spending time alone may lead to spiritual and personal growth. Personal examination may rip you apart and turn you inside out, but after you do the work, the disconcerting, uncomfortable assessment usually brings forth a more refined character and personal authenticity. I must admit that my downtime while in prison was not a voluntary option, but in the end, it became deeply rewarding and spiritually enriching. It provided the time for me to reflect, reconsider, and examine myself and my life. It provided time for me to ask myself, "Where are you going, and why are you destroying your life?"

For the most part, American blacks appear to have little if any belief in the social policies mandated by legislative powers that are theoretically meant to protect all people. The policies may be written with good intentions and they may be imbedded in the laws of the land—in theory created for all—but somehow the policies appear powerless for many blacks.

A good illustration might be a neighborhood store with different shopping times for different segments of the community. These and other, similar types of social paralysis appear more tolerated in southern states, although the pattern is not geographically isolated. Most everyone knows that racial tension and quiet tolerance are present, but they also comprise an elusive and cruel presence. It is cruel because racism learned to disguise itself and give itself a makeover to camouflage its disengaging behavior and racial tendencies. Denying it exists is both the fuel that feeds its fire and the fan that keeps the flames of social disconnect burning, especially (but not exclusively) between blacks and whites.

Like most, I am disturbed about the recent community/law enforcement disruptions because we, as

Americans, regardless of race, creed, or gender, should be far advanced as a people, and our humanity should be an example to the world. One would like to think that our society has grown out of its old divisive and racial differences. The reality is that we have grown, but we have not yet overcome, and we continue to be challenged in our very humanity. From the rampant public spectacle of decades gone by to our modern, "sanitized" social reality today, some of the same challenges still exist in subtle, quiet, and unexpected ways, and in socially acceptable, institutional venues. It is deeply disturbing, a spiritual vexation, and a social disease hiding in plain sight in the fabric of our contemporary democracy.

Social sensitivity workshops have been designed to work through issues and causes of racial divisiveness. Some of them have been successful in bridging the problems while others have not. These types of gatherings are intended to harvest goodwill and inspire the mending of fences and the restoration of trust broken by individual personnel and by law enforcement in general. Still, the workshops cannot be considered as a group discount, like a "groupon" coupon, by which everyone present will receive the same benefits from the class simply by attending. Instead, it is an individual, personal benefit for each person attending such classes to realize their potential inclinations toward racial tolerance and racial equity. Good will has never intended to hurt anyone, but extending or applying less than is needed to meet an urgent need can translate to an overall devastating effect for society.

Until American society is willing to honestly discuss the depths of racial divisiveness with candor and transparency, the problems will continue to escalate before they dissipate. The core or frame of the historical dynamics of racism and bigotry remain at the threshold for healing. The historical, residual effects of the past may have faded with time, but in time the behaviors of racial hate and social resentments have managed to stubbornly resurface through elusive policies and masked expressions of social inequality. Both black and white Americans have witnessed and felt the nasty, detrimental effects of racism and racial divisiveness. Racism should be recognized as a social cancer: elusive, hidden, and sometimes lethal.

Both races must become willing to clean up the mess and messiness involved in dismantling and uprooting the instruments of racism that have encumbered all Americans. Clearly, social liberation is not an easy endeavor by any stretch of the imagination. Racism has become intrinsically institutional and ruthlessly evasive, especially when efforts to engage or eradicate it are employed. It has become highly complex and perplexingly sophisticated within society. It appears to have bunkered in and hunkered down in its fortified mountain, so to speak, resisting any advances to oppose it. Efforts to challenge it continue to be blocked at the foothills, and there seems to be only a small chance of ever making it to the lower slopes, much less advancing all the way to the mountaintop. Could the power of resistance be more homogenously concentrated at the top?

"Do you not know that God's kindness is meant to lead you to repentance? But by your hard and impenitent heart you are storing up wrath for yourself on the day of wrath when God's righteous judgement will be revealed . . . on that day when, according to my gospel, God judges the secrets of men by Christ Jesus" (Romans 2:4b–5, 16).

Understanding the problems of racism has been academically and scientifically documented, but social perception is that this insidious evil is deceptively and dangerously masked. In other words, you cannot fight or access what you can't see, what you can't put your finger on. The reality of racism is well tailored and socially well-tempered, so that denial of its presence almost tends to suggest that it no longer exists. The presence of racism has become well tolerated, which is a subtle denial of its existence, one that may be the most significant cause of the resentment that fuels the physical destructiveness and vindictive social disruptions of violence between law enforcement and communities.

The current damages to our social fabric are not new, but they are deep enough to break the scabs of old, unhealed wounds. Some fights seem necessary and even justified, but racial chaos by nature is a nasty bigot and career criminal that refuses to concede for a better humanity and the moral goodness necessary for a healthy society.

While there are some politicians who are willing to stand up for the humanity they were elected to serve, the public must realize the personal stakes involved in political processes. The ideas of "constituents" and "compromises" are not to be taken lightly, as they have the power and potential to be thorns in the side of even the likes of Lex Luther (Superman's arch nemesis). Words and ideas like peace, justice, right, wrong, fairness, moral strength, goodwill, and good faith appear in the public arena (e.g., in the media) almost as if they are on trial to prove their worth and validity. Words like justice, fairness, human decency, moral conscience, and dignity can make men vulnerable and reveal their *lack* of conscience, moral character, and human dignity. In this way, good faith, if available, can create an adverse reaction that reinforces the lack of moral turpitude.

When there are public servants who are willing to do the right things for the people who make up society, we must stand to encourage and support them. We must stand behind them, but also in front of them to remind them that people and communities are depending on them—and not just their constituents or financial backers.

Social visibility and social perception are two significant areas for harboring contempt between black and white people. It is common sense that there can be no social transformation without intelligent, calm, mature communication—without which the ongoing social unrest and property destruction will only continue to escalate social disruption and deter social cohesion.

How can such improved communication happen? One practical suggestion is that maybe we could listen with intentionality toward solutions that encourage reconciliation rather than misunderstanding each other. Let me say it in another way—we tend to spend more time trying to misunderstand rather than understand each other. There is also need in some instances for blacks to express better respect for themselves and others. Despite how black people may feel they are received by white people, they must socially embrace their rights as Americans to say that America is also theirs. In other words, I am black or dark-skinned, but I am American; whether I am good or not so good, whether I succeed or fail, I am American.

Those who have made the unwise decisions of criminal behavior must also realize that they, too, are still Americans, regardless of having committed a crime. Of course, they have a responsibility to correct the wrongs they have committed, but even persons who have been convicted of felony crimes are still Americans. True, they have broken society's laws, which require punishment to satisfy the need for justice, societal order, and human decency. At the same time, though, penalties must be equally commensurate to the nature, degree, and severity of the crime, not extremes of disproportionate or excessive punishment engineered for protecting political careers and social ascension. When their sentences have been served, or when their time served justifies reasonable parole release, prisoners should be released to return to their normal lives without subordinate labels or epithets that undermine identity. Prisoners must not be abusively mistreated or underrepresented because of bad choices they may (or may not) have made. The tragic reality is that not all prisoners who are locked up have committed crimes—and an even bigger reality is that not all criminals are punished, nor are all criminals locked up.

Because Americans overall tend to favor American ideals as well as home-grown solutions to the nation's unique problems, I believe there is a unique opportunity for American Christians and churches to help heal their own land. After all, Christians share the same land as non-Christians, and Christians often share the same insidious sins as non-Christians, including embedded racism, however well-masked or modernized. Not only that, Christians are convicted of crimes alongside non-Christians. With the humility of both a shared history and social environment and a shared sinfulness, I believe that American Christians are the country's best hope to address its most insidious evils.

I welcome the great American ideal of "One nation under God, with liberty and justice for all," which should become the baseline instrument for appraisal regarding our criminal justice system. One's wrongs or rights should not become their final hymn. Rather than simply labeling a life unworthy and unredeemable as a result of unwise choices, we should be bringing our American values to bear. Instead of the all-too-easy path of blanket condemnation, we should be challenging aggressors to correct their behavior for a better character and discipline.

Justice in the Womb

> Power and those in control concede nothing without a demand. It never did, it never will.[4]
>
> —Fredrick Douglass

Many prisoners are locked up because of inflated police reports at the time of arrest. The arresting officer has the responsibility at the beginning of the arrest to write a truthful arrest report—but he or she also has expansive freedom to increase, exaggerate, or exacerbate the charge. Thus, the arresting officer wields great power during an arrest that can potentially destroy someone's life, resulting in permanent, egregious damage. The arresting officer's report is supposed to be reviewed by a grand jury, which is the legal body that decides if the police report the arresting officer filed has enough merit to bring charges against the suspect. A review of the accuracy of the charges filed by the arresting officer, or how closely they were scrutinized by the grand jury, may or may not be available for the public or even for legal counsel. What

4. AZ Quotes, "Frederick Douglass Quotes," accessed Dec. 24, 2017, http://www.azquotes.com/author/4104-Frederick_Douglass.

is significant at this point of the charging process is that the rightful and true charges are written and filed before the arrest report is given to the court.

This part of any arrest is extremely critical because it has pivotal potential and power to result in a law violator either to be sentenced appropriately or to receive a sentence that is extremely disproportionate, unfair, and unjust. The severity of punishment is based largely on the offense reported by the arresting officer. Justice requires that the time should fit the crime, but there are thousands of men and women incarcerated wholly or in part because of racist, opportunistic, and apathetic police.

No arrest or police report should be arbitrarily conducted without diligent moral honesty and integrity. Critical oversight and review of all criminal charges must be executed by unbiased, unprejudiced, and impartial grand jury panels. The grim reality is that there are thousands of black men incarcerated simply based on the word of one police officer. Prejudice, racial profiling, and social apathy toward black men are invisible strikes, but they are also strikes that count in court. An unspoken reality is that since people no longer can be arrested for being black, it becomes an option for police to invent a violation and call it a crime, or to "upgrade" a crime to make it a worse crime.

> *Criminals, it turns out, are the one social group in America we have permission to hate. . . . They are entitled to no respect and little moral concern. . . . When we say someone was "treated like a criminal," what we mean to say is that he or she was treated as less human. . . . Hundreds of years ago, our nation put those considered less than human in shackles; less than one hundred years ago we relegated them to the other side of town; today we put them in cages. Once released, they find that a heavy and cruel hand has been laid upon them.*[5]
>
> —MICHELLE ALEXANDER

Even if charged accurately, lawbreakers are Americans and should be treated with decency and respect, without negative labeling and social policies designed to crush the life out of them with no chance for recovery or healing. It is quite an issue for a state to punish a person with such severity that they effectively become invisible. The commission of a crime should be subject to punishment, of course, but punishment should also be relative to the offense, mending the breach in the societal fabric with an appropriate repair. The sentencing phase of the justice system has become abusive, insensitive, and vindictive. Understandably, securing justice consistently is an enormous challenge, but for too many black Americans, the sentencing criteria and judicial polemics contain unwritten vengeance codes instigated and propelled by society's reactionary emotions instead of impartiality and objectivity.

5. Alexander, *The New Jim Crow*, 138.

The punishment phase of America's judicial system must be executed appropriately by law enforcement administration, and revenge should be neither implied nor implicit. For our judicial system to be just, there cannot be space for emotions, bigotry, or bias. Unfortunately, even in today's advanced state of jurisprudence, emotions are unavoidably present and influential. While ostensibly looking out for law-abiding citizens, lawmakers cannot help but be influenced by public emotions, and they are writing laws to please the public and public sentiment. Many can agree that the justice system has major issues, but what is the solution for such an embedded and slippery problem such as bias?

For one, blacks have an urgent need to become more visibly involved, both locally and nationally, in the governing processes in their communities. There is an increasingly stronger need to become more proactive in the legislative processes regarding criminal justice and community relations, judges' and prosecutors' elections, and other legal instruments that are potentially helpful, beneficial, and supportive. Blacks must become more engaged amid the governing bodies within their communities.

For another, they must become—socially and judicially—more visible, responsive, and consistent in their protests, but also more responsible. It is both morally decent and noble to speak out when life has been taken by police under questionable circumstances. Too often, unfortunately, such a protest—even when it starts as a simple act of civil disobedience—results in others losing their lives, including policemen and innocent citizens. This creates a vicious cycle of violence breeding more violence, all of which serves to reinforce the biases of those already biased. It should go without saying that engaging law enforcement with the intent to fight physically or with weapons will result in more violence and loss of life. This accomplishes nothing positive, and even puts the progress engine in reverse for blacks.

> *I think I am in agreement with most of the Judges in the federal system that mandatory minimums are an imprudent, unwise, and often unjust mechanism for sentencing.*[6]
>
> —SUPREME COURT JUSTICE ANTHONY KENNEDY, 1994

Blacks are aware of the legal processes for social redress and reform; the process is not the problem. The problem is the *time* it takes for the judicial system to be reformed. The processes of renovating our monolithic system have been shown to take too long and to involve endless delays, all of which only serve to frustrate an already frustrated people. The sense of judicial apathy becomes a resident nemesis to the process—in other words, the system is the system's own worst enemy.

Social differences of race and class will probably always be a nuisance for some people because personal

6. Joel Dyer, *The Perpetual Prisoner Machine: How America Profits from Crime* (Boulder, CO: Westview Press, 2000), 153.

feelings cannot be subject to legislation. The focus should be on changing the laws and, more importantly, preventing some proposed bills from ever becoming laws.

It is the overreach and inherent injustice of certain laws that frustrate, anger, and incite public redress. Judges and prosecutors will only exercise their authority as far as the legal code allows, but many laws, as written, subtly allow for improper justice. This is where being informed and involved in the legislative process becomes so important. It is in the processes of writing laws where society's voices should be heard most loudly. The social protest should be loudest in the legislative chambers, not primarily on the streets, and especially not only after someone has been taken from their loved ones. By then, the system has already failed. And when such protests turn violent themselves, the system regresses and becomes even more reactionary and emotional. For the entire body of justice to be reformed, it must be addressed at a much more embryonic stage than after it has given birth to injustice. Justice must begin at the conception stage; it must be nurtured in the womb of the legislative process.

It is not my intention to sound demeaning or critical of blacks. Of course, many blacks *are* socially and politically involved, both behind the scenes and on the cutting edge of politics, law enforcement, and social venues within society. My hope is to heighten the urgency and desperate need of more black people to become more involved and engaged in the inner and formative processes of criminal justice, which alone has a viable chance of creating change prior to the distribution and execution of its power. When that system fails, as it inevitably does at times, they need to respond with renewed commitment to clear but nonviolent protest, while simultaneously digging in deeper at the legislative and formative levels. They also need to become more involved at all stages of the execution of justice, including becoming cops, corrections officers, probation and parole officers, pre- and post-release counselors, chaplains, and all the many social worker, child welfare, and countless other positions along the collective journey toward restorative justice.

Finally, above all, biblical wisdom must dominate the landscape of a renewed vision for criminal justice reform. Perhaps even better than reform are the concepts of restoring, returning, and renewing our own reliance on biblical principles as the source of our leadership and the strength of our faith in our Lord Jesus Christ—which, in turn, will help renew and redeem the broken offender. I believe that true rehabilitation includes restoring, renewing, and returning to the biblical fundamentals that gave birth to the principles and integrity of a people united under obedience and reverence toward our spiritual formation, and which define our Christian character as Americans.

In the courtroom, it is our Christian heritage and integrity that takes the stand, which is why one hand is placed on the Bible and the other hand is raised in reverence to our Lord in honor of our Christian faith. Maybe we should revisit just what or who is to be rehabilitated—is it our wrongs or our Christian values? As Mahatma Gandhi once said, "I like your Christ, I do not like your Christians. Your Christians are so unlike your Christ."[7] The Bible words it like this: "My friends, if anyone is detected in a transgression, you who have received the Spirit should restore such a one in a spirit of gentleness" (Galatians 6:1).

---

7. Good Reads, "Mahatma Ghandi Quotes," accessed Jan. 13, 2017, https://www.goodreads.com/quotes/22155-i-like-your-christ-i-do-not-like-your-christians.

CHAPTER II

THE HOLES WE DIG IN OUR LIVES ARE THE HOLES WE MUST DIG OUT OF

Dig It Out

> Lord, we pray for tranquility, not that our tribulations may cease; we pray for THY Spirit and THY Love that thou grant us strength and grace to overcome adversity.[8]
>
> —Girolamo Savonarola

A significant block of people exist who are in the custody of the criminal justice system, and the system will not release them even after they are set free. Whether they are on parole or enrolled in some type of chemical dependence or life skills program, their lives continue to be governed by the state, which constitutes criminal justice oversight over them. According to the *Dallas News*, as of July 31, 2016, there were 146,843 inmates in Texas prisons. The same article stated that "Black and Latino men make up more than three-fifths of the [US] prison population, including two-thirds of those locked up in Texas' 109 facilities.[9] According to TDCJ's annual Statistical

8. Girolamo Savonarola, unknown source.
9. James Ragland, "If Texas' Prison Population Were a City, it Would Be the State's 20th Largest," *Dallas News* (Sept 2016), accessed Jan. 15, 2018, https://www.dallasnews.com/opinion/commentary/2016/09/16/texas-prison-population-city-states-20th-largest.

Report, those under state supervision totaled 374,980 in 2016, among whom blacks and Latinos comprised more than 50 percent.[10] I believe that a significant percentage of these could be productive citizens, but those who are living successful post-incarceration lives make up only a small percentage of the nearly 70,000 who are released from prison in Texas each year.[11] Despite the obstacles, a small number of persons have successfully recaptured their lives after incarceration and have stretched themselves into a new life. I say stretched because it is not easy, starting over in life after incarceration, carrying the stigma that permanently brands a person. It is like taking a shower over and over but never getting clean.

When someone is released from prison, of course they are extremely happy and feel wonderful—even brand new! They get to see and visit people and relatives whom they have not seen for a while, and some not for quite a long time. They savor the blessing to eat their favorite dinners, pies, and cakes. They relish the luxury to drink a second glass of tea or orange juice, maybe a sip of wine or beer. They get to wear new clothes, because even if they are second-hand, they are new to someone who has worn prison whites for a long time (different states have different colors). They cherish the simple joys of riding in a car

10. Texas Department of Criminal Justice Statistical Report (FY 2016), accessed Jan. 15, 2018, https://www.tdcj.state.tx.us/documents/Statistical_Report_FY2016.pdf.
11. Release rate from Texas Criminal Justice Coalition, "Parole and Reentry," accessed Dec. 21, 2017, https://www.texascjc.org/parole-reentry.

and listening to music at the same time—and it's the type of music they choose to listen to.

In a sense, they feel like teenagers again, excited that they can now stay out late (if they are not on a monitor), and that they are free to have a girlfriend again. Life as they once knew it begins to come back to them, like riding a bike again after many years. It feels good, being out of prison. They can live and do what they want to without someone telling them what to do and when to do it. Some may thank and praise God for their freedom and some may not. For many, the feeling of being at home or just being free can be shocking and overwhelming to their system, especially those who have been incarcerated for a very long time. There are stores, shopping malls, cell phones, clothes, new styles and trends, new language, and many new devices with which to get acquainted. It's fun, it's fascinating, it's all good!

At the same time, however, as has often been said, along with freedom comes responsibilities. They must not forget to check in with their parole officer, which is okay because they are free. Hopefully, they will be assigned to a decent parole officer, but all parole officers will clearly inform them of their dos and don'ts. Some things on the list may feel like they're spoiling that freedom to some, while others won't mind. Freedom for all who have lost it is of the greatest importance, and it means more than anything or anybody at this point to those who have been released from prison. In this light, the trips to the parole office are okay, and they wait patiently to be picked up and returned by whomever brought them. The word "Thanks!" becomes prevalent in their vocabulary and takes on an entirely new meaning.

A few days go by, and then a few weeks, and then a few months pass, all of which is good of course, simply because the person is still free. But what about the job he was supposed to get? One of the conditions of parole is to get a job, and he has not been able to find one. Why is getting a job so difficult when he thought work would be rather easy to find? He wonders what he has done to not deserve to get a job when he really wants to work. Isn't an honest job what everyone always wanted him to have? He realizes that he never even considered the possibility that finding a job—any job—would be this difficult.

In *The New Jim Crow*, Alexander articulates well the plight of the paroled:

> He will also be told little or nothing about the parallel universe he is about to enter, one that promises a form of punishment that is often more difficult to bear than prison time: a lifetime of shame, contempt, scrod, and exclusion. In this hidden world, discrimination is perfectly legal. As Jeremy Travis has observed, "In this brave new world, punishment for the original offense is no longer enough; one's debt to society is never paid." Other commentators liken the prison label to "the mark

> of Cain" and characterize the perpetual nature of the sanction as "internal exile."[12]

Because of this "invisible punishment," parolees are "unable to surmount these obstacles" and "most will eventually return to prison and then be released again, caught in a closed circuit of perpetual marginality."[13]

What does the thinking of a parolee sound like? Let's revisit the "new life of freedom" of the average parolee mentioned in chapter 1.

Locked In—Which Way Is Out?

> No man can put a chain about the ankle of his fellow man without at last finding the other end fastened about his own neck.[14]
>
> —Frederick Douglass

You have been out of prison five months and still have no job, and the parole officer begins to get at you about being a little tough to work with. You begin to get upset because of the tone of his conversation, but then he calls you angry. That judgment call of his goes somewhere you did not think it could, but you find yourself having real anger issues, and now you are required to attend anger

12. Alexander, *The New Jim Crow*, 139.

13. Ibid., 181.
14. From a speech at a Civil Rights Mass Meeting, Washington, DC, 22 Oct. 1883. AZ Quotes, "Frederick Douglass Quotes," accessed Dec. 24, 2017, http://www.azquotes.com/author/4104-Frederick_Douglass.

management classes. It seems unreasonable, but it is also unreasonable that you are told to just do as you are told to do—or else! That last phrase has a lot of emphasis on it. Be careful! Be very careful at this point in your life, because the joys of your freedom just might be at stake. Be careful! Not all parole officers are the same, just as not all people are the same, but you must realize the weight of the situation is on you, and your self-discipline becomes imperative.

Everything continues to go well and you have the peace of not being employed while you continue to look for work, but it has been nine months and you still have not landed a job. The parole officer continues to work with you and may even offer some peaceful resolve and understanding, but the problem is not the parole officer. The problem is at home, or whatever your living arrangement may be. Trouble where you live disturbs your peace and creates anxiety, but you think you can weather the storm. A few weeks later, you hope you can weather the storm, and then a couple of months after that, you decide the storms are coming too often, so you consider moving somewhere else. You think hard about things, and for a minute it seems like the storms are dissipating, but then a hurricane blows up over you and tosses you around with shouts of what you have not done and what you ought to be doing. You are reminded where you came from, and that you wouldn't be living where you are if it wasn't for someone else taking you in . . . as if you are nothing . . .

and then you are reminded that you don't have anything to give anyone anyway.

You realize for the first time in a long time that you have a choice now. You can stay there and accept being scorned and belittled like a child with no respect, or you may leave, and so you decide to leave. After making up your mind, you decide where you may go, but you realize it is not that easy. You must get permission from the parole officer before you can move. That may not be a problem, but you do have to get permission . . . and then you do, and you leave his office thinking, wow, that went okay!

So you move and begin to find your way in life, and you begin to enjoy being free again. Maybe a year has passed, and you did finally get a job, but it doesn't pay enough. The job only pays minimum wage, and you begin to think that you will never get ahead on what you are making. You may ask for a raise and get it, but even with the raise what you take home is still insufficient. There are things you want to buy and have, and there are places you want to go, but on the type of wages you are earning it's not going to happen. So you begin to look for another job while tentatively holding on to the job you have. A bird in the hand is better than a bird in the bushes. You are starting to use wisdom!

Finally, you do get another job that pays a little more, and you think you even like it better than the last job. Then things begin to happen again where you live, but this time it is about not paying enough rent. You begin to pay more rent, but you realize the rent is taking too much of your money, so you want to protest but you don't want to incite an argument. You begin to feel trapped again. What will you do?

As you begin living your newly chosen way of life, you are inevitably faced with all the post-release realities the parole counselors did not tell you about, which gradually begin to make you angry. You understand that you are not angry with yourself, but rather that you are angry with the entire criminal justice system. You were not prepared for the after-thoughts—you assumed that freedom would overpower your bad memories. Yet the more time passes, the more you begin to think of all the days and nights you went to sleep hungry, and how you were treated—and mistreated. You begin to relive a litany of all the mean and disrespectful ways you were treated while you were incarcerated. You become that much angrier, and you begin to rationalize and justify your anger.

You might tell yourself that you have a right to be angry. You begin to feel isolated and held back in life simply because you have been to prison. You begin to realize that you are still a prisoner of sorts, because you are locked into a system that feeds off your demise and the self-destructive feelings of being just another nameless, faceless statistic caught up in the system—a system you naively thought was there to help you get your life back in order. Now you begin to see reality more clearly, and you realize both that the system expects you to fail and that the deck is stacked against you.

At first, you feel like the overly general cliché "victim of the system," but you realize that the reality is much more nuanced and subtle. You realize there is no "pursuit of life and liberty" in most instances for post-release offenders. You cannot vote while on parole, or you must wait two years past your last imprisonment, but there is no waiting period for paying taxes—which could be alleviated or at least modified to assist in the process of reentering society.

Housing and government assistance are not available in most instances, or they are more difficult to receive than people think. Employment is difficult to accomplish because of your felony conviction, which is a stigma that will follow you forever. Countless highly qualified non-offenders express in all forms of media the struggle to find work. The news is filled with statistics about high unemployment, which sometimes is captured with the expression "PhDs becoming baristas" and other examples of a struggling economy. How does someone with a record compete?

As well, the men and women suffering as prolonged prisoners of the parole system (in legal terms, they are still under the custody of the state) are constantly reminded of the potential threat of returning to prison while on parole. There are some causes that lead to revocation or violation of parole that are valid violations—but many other things that violate parole for offenders and send them back to prison could easily be mitigated (see the sidebar at the end of this passage).

Like the late, great poet Marvin Gaye said, "You go to the place where danger awaits you, self-destructions in your hands . . . and you know you are hooked on something that makes slaves out of men." You say you are not going back—"I can handle it. I am a man"—but your actions do not reflect those of a man.

What your conscience speaks to you is the truth you choose not to hear, and you refuse to yield to the plea your own conscience tried to appeal to you with. What you did not want to hear is exactly what you heard deep down in your soul. The truth you knew and grievously crushed out of your mind was that if you step on that ground, it is not holy but rather holes in the ground. You knew you were on your way back to where you swore you would never go back to. The minute your "hook up" put that trash in your hands you felt like trash, but you sucked up some good yet wasted air into your nostrils, because you knew you were only breathing up your new-found hell.

And you were the one who rode the bus there.

You Dug Your Own Hole

> When a great truth gets abroad in the world, no power on earth can imprison it, or prescribe its limits, or suppress it. It is bound to go on till it becomes the thought of the world.[15]
>
> —Frederick Douglass

15. Frederick Douglass, Philip Sheldon Foner, and Yuval Taylor, *Frederick Douglass: Selected Speeches and Writings* (Chicago: Chicago Review Press, 1999), 710.

People with criminal records face a daunting array of challenges. Without a job, it is impossible to provide for oneself and one's family. Without a driver's license, it is harder to land or keep a job. Without affordable housing or food stamps or federal monies to participate in alcohol or drug treatment, it is harder to lead a stable, productive life. Without the right to vote, the ability to adopt or raise foster children, or access to a college loan, it is harder to become a fully engaged citizen in the mainstream of society. These roadblocks block the reintegration of people with criminal records, which in turn compromises everyone's safety and the well-being of our communities.[16]

—NEW YORK LEGAL ACTION CENTER

Of course, some violations indeed are serious and deserving of a return to prison, but others are minor infractions, and some, if we are honest, stem from an exaggerated miscommunication or a perceived attitude of angry temperament. A common saying is, "You dug your own hole," meaning that the person has earned everything that happens after a criminal conviction. While this, of course, applies during the incarceration phase of the consequences for breaking the law, when does it end? Do police have the right to become aggressive, for example, for no other reason than that they found out someone has a record? Someone could be charged with violating his parole for "resisting arrest" when a policeman monitoring a speed trap, for example, becomes aggressive and intimidating,

16. Legal Action Center, "After Prison: Roadblocks to Reentry, A Report on State Legal Barriers Facing People with Criminal Records" (New York: Legal Action Center, 2004), accessed Jan. 5, 2018, www.lac.org/roadblocks.html, 23.

provoking the parolee by pushing his human buttons until he reacts badly. No one else witnesses his "resistance," and no one will question the officer's word, so no matter how well the ex-offender was doing, his parole is revoked and he returns to prison.

With so many social opportunities unavailable to offenders, their chances of gaining a successful and happy life often devolve into circumstances of extreme hopelessness and deteriorating optimism. The situation is extremely sad and cruel because it sends the message to the offenders that the system has no positive regard for their lives, that no matter what they did or how long ago they did it, they in effect received a life sentence. This situation reminds me of the period when the slaves were set free, but there was no place for them to go and be free. There was simply no place where they could live as free people and pursue a new life of their own. Why do so many men go back to prison? It is not because they are expected to dig themselves out of their own hole, the one for which they are responsible, as often they accept that responsibility and are willing to do the digging. Rather, it is because they are expected to dig themselves out of an infinitely bigger hole that society has dug for them, a hole that has no bottom.

Who would trust them? Who would receive them? What were their chances of living a successful life? This type of freedom could become more of a burden than liberation, more of an invisible minefield than a long-awaited relief from having paid their debt to society. Could this situation be the secret to the modern slave master's plan regarding the concept of reentry? In theory, reentry programming and initiatives were implemented to facilitate a better chance for successful reintegration into society. Sadly, even essential resources are often not available upon release, and if it were not for caring volunteers making themselves available on day one of release, many offenders would not make it a week as free people. In the real world, opportunities that sound good on paper are often unavailable to the offenders when they get off the bus with their $50 check in hand. The truth that no one wants to hear is that the door of reentry swings both ways with equal ease—reentry into society, and reentry into prison.

It should be self-evident that persons reentering society require essential resources such as human necessities. It should be an obvious reality that they will face more challenges resulting from the stigma of incarceration, and the public predictably will alienate itself from them. Even those who consider themselves trusting people will be more distant and more reluctant to receive or accept most people coming out of prison. This response is familiar to those coming out of the system because they are more aware than anyone of the stigmatizing labels that weigh heavily on their lives as ex-offenders.

A successful reentry program must have five essential resources available to all offenders: housing, employment assistance, clothes, life skills classes, and supportive community assistance (community visibility). Unfortunately, the system leaves arrangements for these types of necessities to churches and charitable ministries. Indeed, it may be more accurate to say that churches are partners in the resocialization of offenders. At the same time, doing so places the monetary burden on churches, and because most in these ministries are volunteers, it also places the untrained to work with a population of people they probably do not really know how to access or understand. By default, they are often the only ones willing to become involved, and that is highly commendable, but at the same time, their intervention skills might be limited.

The basic human needs of personal hygiene, such as toothpaste, deodorant, soap, cleaning supplies, or the meager money it takes to purchase them, are so easily overlooked as minor needs, but they are real burdens for any person starting over in life, especially without family support. As well, there are other urgent and bigger needs, including housing, employment assistance, food, clothing, training, and so on—all of which are burdens both for the reentering individual and people who are not trained or properly prepared to realistically assess the post-release needs of offenders.

Economic inequalities often lead to involvement with drugs, which often leads to incarceration—and these three dynamics are the primary contributors facilitating the demise of the black man. Starting from economic desperation, I believe that turning to drugs for quick cash and the resulting incarceration are the two major villains behind the degeneration and lack of social mobility for black men. After that, a felony conviction becomes yet another burden to carry, and it will just about break his back and could cause him to re-offend (reentry in reverse) or return to the old environment of criminal and aberrant behavior. This quickly becomes the vicious cycle discussed earlier.

For some men, life on the outside seems hopeless and opportunities are limited, either because of their felony conviction or because there was no one present in their life to offer them healthy guidance and positive direction. Offenders are familiar with the phrase "starting in the middle," which is the juggling act of having one foot at home and one foot in a destructive environment. Consequently, for some men, starting their new life from the middle is normal. The obvious question to be asked and answered is: how and why does any man restart his life in the middle? How did they get there, and how could they have avoided it? What are some of the dynamics that have caused the middle start for so many black men? It is as simple as the societal double-bind they experience, that they dug their own hole so they need to dig their own way out—but society prefers that they remain in the hole, digging indefinitely.

There has been a lot of analysis about the causes of recidivism, and there are many well-reasoned proposals about how to address and resolve issues like these that plague our society. In the end, though, it seems like they tend to center on the minor details, focusing on symptoms rather than the systemic heart of the problem. The point for the black man to comprehend is, how does he respond to the pitfalls of a life of freedom without basic positive regard for himself, which society projects on him through negative lenses? Unfortunately, too many have responded by rejecting the analyses and instead have adopted a frame of mind more hazardous to themselves than inspiring.

Of course, the black man is not immune to society's overall shallow values, which leads him to believe that what he has is what he is worth. A subtle message he may learn from society is that what he may or may not accomplish will depend more on his color than his capabilities. Competence and capabilities are harvested through academic achievements, but unfortunately for many black men, the idea of education is not on their list of priorities. This may or may not be because they are not academically competent enough to become educated, but in too many instances it is because there simply was no healthy father/mother relationship in their life to encourage them in the right direction. All young men need someone available for them, in whom they can trust to guide them in ways that inspire them toward healthy, attainable goals and aspirations. Otherwise, they are susceptible to the culture at large, which typically inspires them to value certain negative things that some young men think are the attributes of a man.

It should go without saying that there are many successful black men in the world. Another obvious reality that seems to need repeating is that there are too many black men, women, and youth warehoused in prisons and jails, especially in Texas. Of course, Texas takes pride in everything being big in Texas, but is it a good thing that the state has the largest prison system in the nation, with more than 150,000 inmates in more than 100 prisons and state jails? Statistics reflect that there are fewer black offenders incarcerated in Texas than white, Hispanic, and others, but there is a disproportionate number of black offenders based on race populations in the state. Is it because blacks are inherently worse people—or is it because they are inherently disadvantaged, with fewer good choices while growing up and becoming young adults?

Regardless of race, men and women who have been incarcerated continue to be marginalized, labeled, and misjudged because of their past behavior and past incarceration. Even if they are 100 percent rehabilitated, how do they overcome society's entrenched bias against them? They are compelled to learn to accept fewer opportunities to pursue a better life and future because their felony conviction has impeached most of their chances for them to succeed in life. This type of mentality has become all too familiar within black communities. Commission of any crime is wrong, and often incarceration is the appropriate and necessary punishment for both justice and public safety. There is a thin line, however, between just and appropriate punishment and all the many forms of inappropriate punishment, including subtle but systemic and historical bias against black offenders and the inherent life sentence of having a record.

There have been countless discussions about prisons and people who go to prison—discussions about equity in sentencing, early release options, crime dynamics and statistics, appropriate punishments, deterrents, various types of supervision, etc. I have been actively engaged with prisons and prison ministry for most of my life, first as an inmate, and then in prison ministry. In more than fifty years of hands-on involvement, I have witnessed only minimal rehabilitation. It seems to be difficult to determine what is effective and what is not effective because the custodians of criminals and those who write the mandates for them universally want more money to build more prisons and jails, not to mention the additional staff and maintenance needed. In its checkered history, the Texas prison system has resembled a complex conglomerate with an insurance agency mentality.

How do so many black men, women, and youth become locked up in the first place? Did they get up one morning and decide to fill up all the jails and prisons because prison/jail hospitality is simply too good to pass up? Is the breakfast that good? I once read a T-shirt that had the slogan that Texas prisons have a pretty good bed and bath. Did they get up one morning and decide to become a drug addict because it was the best thing on the market? Did they get up one morning and decide to go to hell because that is where all the good times are? Did they get up one morning and decide to have more babies than they could afford and leave their wives and girlfriends with the bills and responsibilities? Did they wake up and decide to become a deadbeat father with low self-esteem and no education? Did they wake one morning and figure out there was no employment suitable for them? Did they wake up one morning with hell in them and decide to pay hell's rent to take up residence there? Did they plan a vacation to hell?

Studies have shown that it often appears as if black men think going to jail or prison was always just around the corner anyway. There was one study that revealed that criminal authorities and lawmakers negotiate with the private prison industry to build prisons based on the rate of third grade dropouts. One of the common defenses for this mentality is, "It is what it is." While I fully understand the meaning of the phrase, I simply refuse to give it any legitimacy or substance. In fact, I would respond with a familiar saying of my own, "The only constant is change," and there is no reason why this cannot apply to the criminal justice system.

What is ironic is that people often complain that prisoners receive more benefits than they deserve. Yet even when they are finished serving their time, no matter the actual conditions of the unit, they invariably struggle to connect with the necessary resources that would support and enhance their opportunity for a successful reentry. At some indefinable point in time, it's as if it became socially acceptable to treat them like outcasts, not just for the length of their sentence, parole, or probation, but for life. It doesn't seem to matter if they earned a college degree behind bars, learned highly technical skills, or have effectively been rehabilitated (and Texas, to its credit, does a better job at this than any other state, with a 21 percent recidivism rate at the time of writing). The grim reality that far too many experience upon release is that once they carry the label "ex-offender," they seem to have acquired a disease during their incarceration dating back to biblical times—they became modern day lepers.

Now, having expressed some of my observations and conclusions about some of the grim realities of the criminal justice system, it is time to tell my story so the reader can see where these thoughts started and how my thinking evolved over time.

CHAPTER III

LOST—MY STORY

One and God is a majority.[17]

—Frederick Douglass

As a young boy, between the ages of five and twelve years old, I wanted to be a preacher. My mother told me that she had heard about me from God and that I would become a preacher. My mother passed when I was three years old, but I still remember what she told me I was supposed to do in life. One day, though, my life and social environment abruptly changed, and it was not a good relocation for me as a kid.

Between the ages of nine and thirteen, I had an established church membership at Lilly Grove Missionary Baptist Church in southwest Houston. Even though I was a kid, I was one of the founding members of the church, and I had a very good relationship with the pastor, his family, and the congregation. It was like a second home to me; I spent most of my time there when I was not at school or at home, and I truly enjoyed it. If I could be there during the day, I would be there.

At about age thirteen and a half, my sister—who raised me after my mother and father passed away—told

17. AZ Quotes, "Frederick Douglass Quotes," accessed Dec. 24, 2017, http://www.azquotes.com/quote/81111.

me that I could no longer attend that church because we would be joining a Methodist church in a couple of weeks. I asked if I could continue to attend the Baptist church, but she did not want me to go. I pleaded with her, but she would not change her mind. The pastor of the Baptist church came by our house to try and talk with my sister about the situation, but she said that I was not going back to that church because she wanted the family to attend church together. I attempted to visit the Baptist church between the times I would attend the Methodist church, going back and forth so I could honor my sister's wishes but still get a taste of the church I really enjoyed. One Sunday, I was walking to attend services at the Methodist church across the park when I noticed two older guys with whom I was familiar who were smoking marijuana. They invited me to smoke with them and I did . . . and I never made it to church. Before long, my zeal and enthusiasm began to fade away for attending any church, and I did not return for a very long time.

I believe that this was the beginning of my troubled life. A lot of men who have similar tales do not want this part of their story to be heard because they are ashamed to admit that family may have served as the impetus to their troubled life. When I was told that I could no longer attend the Baptist church I loved, it was spiritually devastating to me. It tore deeply into my soul because I felt like that was the part in me that connected me to my mother. It was my personal relationship with Jesus as I knew him.

I knew him as my Savior, and that part of me was cruelly ripped out of me. No one ever has the right to do that to anyone, and age is not a factor in Jesus Christ. It reconnected me to church and my mother's father, my grandfather, who was a preacher in Marshall, Texas. Herein were my lost years with Christ; I lost my way.

After my father passed, when I was still young, my youngest sister and I lived with our grandparents during the summer months. I really enjoyed living with my grandparents, and especially listening to my grandfather preach. Every evening after supper, he would take me with him to the back of the shed—which for many boys meant whippings, but for me it was for education. There, he would teach me about the gospels—which were interesting, but I wanted to play and make the most of the sunshine before night came. But between my mother and my grandfather, I was right where I was supposed to be—in church. It seemed right, especially since my mother told me that I was supposed to be a preacher, and that her father's church was perfect in every way.

After my sister and her husband came to pick up me and my youngest sister one summer, we were told that we would not go back to live with our grandparents, though we would still visit them from time to time. I wanted to move back in with my grandparents, but my sister and her husband said no. I cried, and even tried to jump out of the car, but my brother held on to me.

That period of time, after I went back to Houston, and as I tried to become acclimated with family and going to school, was when I started going to the Baptist church that my sister later decided she did not want me to continue attending. I attended the Lilly Grove for about two or three years until I was no longer allowed to go. I really enjoyed being a part of that church. I enjoyed the services (mostly watching the preacher preach), and it was at that church where I not only felt reconnected with my mother and grandfather, but also with my mission. As mentioned, I was where I was supposed to be. I was on my way toward serving in the Kingdom of God. When the church was dedicated, I served as the Masonic sacrificial lamb. The Masons spoke over me with their hands laid on my head. I did not understand what they were saying, but I was sure it was something good.

I attended the Methodist church from time to time, but I was deeply unhappy—not because it was a Methodist church, but because I wanted to be at the Baptist church. I had friends there, and they made me feel like family. At the age of thirteen, I did not know any difference between denominations or the meaning of them. What I did know was that I was not happy at home because of some differences between the two churches.

Within a few months of my sister's decision, my favorite brother, James, came home from the Marines and Vietnam. He had become my hero, and I looked up to him with great admiration. He was always my favorite brother, the one who taught me how to play baseball and basketball, but he also taught me some things that were not good.

One day, he showed me some marijuana, and when I told him that I had smoked it with some guys in the park once before, he gave it to me. Looking back, I know my brother meant me no harm, and I know he loved me, but it was not the right thing to give a kid. That was the beginning of what led me to drug abuse.

My sister and her husband became unfriendly toward my brother after a while, and one day they had a big fight, and my sister told him to leave and to take me with him. We both left and I stayed with my brother, but only for a short time. I started living from house to house, between relatives and friends. It wasn't long before I became a drug abuser, homeless, a thug, and a very lost soul. When I could not stay at someone's home, I stayed inside school rooms that were detached from the larger building, or sometimes I slept in parks or door corridors where no one, or at least no cars, could see me. When I realized that I had worn out my welcome among schoolmates and friends, I began to drift even further from my social environment where I grew up. I started sleeping in Herman Park. One night, as I was walking the streets, I discovered a building with a cross and flame on the front of the building. That emblem made me stop and I stared at it, reflecting where I had seen it before. It took me a few minutes, but I remembered that I had seen it at St. Mary's Methodist Church, where my sister wanted our family to go.

I stared at the emblem and then I walked up to it and touched it with my hands. I sat down on the door corridor of that building for a long time that night, and thereafter I would go over to that building and visit the cross and the flame. Because the building faced the street (Main St.) and cars would go by on that busy street too often, I wouldn't sit there too long because I did not want to be discovered. From there, I found a more secluded corridor behind the Museum of the Arts, as it was named at that time. But while I roamed in that vicinity, I would intentionally go over to the building to visit the cross and the flame. I did not know what building it was at that time, but I loved looking at that cross and flame. Much, much later in my life, I learned the building was The Annual Conference of the United Methodist Church.

I share that story because I want to convey how family, social, and psychological dynamics all impact our lives, especially for youth, and may cause some kids to lose their way in life. Breaking away from church shattered my life into pieces. Remembering that cross and flame, and remembering my grandfather's church, I wanted to go back to the church, but I wouldn't go back home. In my kid's mind, I could not bring myself to face the congregation.

I was dirty and hungry most of the time. I was a drug user, depraved, and reckless. I was hurting. I missed my mother, and took pride in believing that if my mother were alive, I would be at home and I would be loved. But my mother was not there, and that reality made me feel cold and mean. I could feel my heart freezing. A broken heart becomes a broken life.

From that point on, I began to get arrested and go to jail for various offenses until finally I went to prison when I was about nineteen. I went to the Ferguson unit in Lovelady, Texas, for three and a half years. Nothing really happened there that is worth talking about here. I really did not learn anything significant; I was only locked up. After I got out of prison, I stayed out for maybe two years.

I continued to smoke weed and drink beer every day. I worked at Piccadilly Cafeteria on and off for a few years, which is where I met my first wife. She was a good wife and a good person who tried to make our marriage work. I was the one who was undecided about life and how I wanted to live my life. I had no focus in life; I had no goals or aspirations. I got married because I thought it would help me stay out of trouble, but it did not. No one else can keep you out of trouble but yourself. Drinking became a problem for me, and I started getting arrested for DWIs and driving with a suspended license. I think I was arrested for drinking and driving about four times. My wife and I began to argue most of the time about my drinking until we separated and finally were divorced. She left me living in the apartment we had shared. Her aunt was the manager of the apartments and she really cared for me.

A Prison Vision

My ex-wife's aunt began to tell me that she was having visits from the Lord about me, and that he had not revealed to her what he wanted me to know, but she was sure it was about me. She told me about it a few more times, and one night, about 2:40 a.m., she came and knocked on my door and I let her in. I asked her what she wanted and she said, "Baby, the good Lord just left my bedside and told me to come and tell you that you are going back to prison for a long time."

I laughed and said, "How long, two years?" She said longer than that.

I said, "What, five years?" She said longer than that.

I said again, "Ten, twelve years?" And she said longer than that.

I said, "I know it can't be any longer than fifteen years." And she said longer than that.

I said, "You are crazy and out of your mind. That isn't for me, that is just some dream you had, but it was not about me."

She looked at me and said, "Marvin, he said you, he called your name." She said, "The Lord don't lie, baby," and went back home.

A few weeks later, on a Saturday evening, I was coming down the steps of the apartment to go out on the town. She was standing at the foot of the stairs, looking down, but when I reached the bottom of the stairs she looked up at me and said, "If you don't go back upstairs and stay in that house, you won't come back here tonight."

I laughed and said, "What are you talking about"?

She said it again, "Marvin, if you leave this house tonight, you won't come back."

I laughed and went on to my car and drove away. About three o'clock in the morning, after I got in trouble, I called my ex-wife's aunt, and when she answered the telephone, she did not say hello, but just said, "Marvin, you are in jail and you will not get out for a long, long time. You are going back to prison." She said, "Marvin, when you get there you will see Jesus; he will speak to you, baby." She added, "If you just remember me, I will get my blessing."

I told her I was arrested for a misdemeanor charge of unauthorized use of a motor vehicle, and that I would be out in a few days.

She said, "Not this time, baby. You will be there a long time."

I asked how long, and she asked me how old I was. I told her, and she said, "You'll get out when you are in your early forties." I was twenty-two when she told me that.

She said to me that nothing could move me and nothing would get me out. She said, "Marvin, you are right where the Lord wants you."

I said, "I have a few people I can call to get me out again."

She said, "You are under the power of the Lord and you will not get out until he is ready to let you out."

I laughed. As it happened, though, the charge I thought I was arrested for was not the charge I had when I went to court. There, I learned that I had been charged with aggravated robbery with a deadly weapon. There had been no gun because I did not have a gun, and I had not touched the complainant. He had been inside of a store and I had not interacted with him at all. He had left his car door open with the keys in it and the motor running. My own car had fallen dead several times (it was an old, ragged, used-up cab). So, I got in the man's car and drove away. According to the trial transcript and testimony of the police, I was arrested eleven minutes after driving away with the car. The district attorney offered me fifteen years, but I was trying to tell him that I did not rob anybody and that it was the wrong charge against me. He said, "Take the fifteen years and you'll probably be out in three."

I said, "I did not rob that man; I drove away with his car."

The district attorney said again, "Take the fifteen because you are a second offender, and if you choose a jury trial, I will throw you away. The aggravated law is brand new, and if you do not take the fifteen, I promise the jury will believe me and not you."

I said, "No." By five o'clock, I was found guilty of aggravated robbery with a deadly weapon and sentenced to ninety-nine years in prison. There was no weapon and no other witnesses than the complainant. I never put my hands on him. There was never a gun. I drove off with his car and the ride lasted twenty years and sixty-one days. I went to prison at the age of twenty-two, and I was released from prison at the age of forty-two. My ex-wife's aunt was right.

In 1977, I started my ninety-nine-year sentence in the Texas Department of Corrections (later changed to Texas Department of Criminal Justice). I was assigned to the worst prison in the state of Texas, according to the Oct. 6, 1986 issue of *Newsweek* magazine: the Eastham prison unit in Lovelady, Texas. I was bitter and angry. I was deeply broken and I felt like my life was over. For a while, I hardly talked to anyone. I did not talk because I was busy talking to myself, trying to make sense out of what had happened to me. How does anyone get ninety-nine years for stealing a car? I kept asking myself this question over and over, but there were no answers.

Then, I began to revisit some of the accidental guests I had encountered at different times in my life. They were just ordinary people, but things were different now, and this time they were people with a message meant for me.

TDCJ's Rehabilitation Program Division (RPD)

The above-mentioned *Newsweek* article, which accurately captured the state of TDC during the time of my incarceration, also captured the beginning of sweeping reforms that gradually saturated the entire agency. It wasn't a smooth process, but it was a necessary process, because ultimately, the bulk of inmates will be released, and how they leave prison ultimately determines whether their incarceration experience will have a positive effect on society. According to the article:

> Such are the disorderly lessons of reform, several steps forward and different steps back, many lives helped, others damaged and some lost. In other words, reform imitates life, demanding will and zeal—and humility. But resignation seems a less deplorable alternative, ethically and practically. For prisons that operate utterly isolated from view, by abhorrent codes of conduct, can become dark and vicious places. And that's reason enough to promote order and change in institutions that lock in cages men who will eventually return to our streets.[18]

18. Pedersen, Shapiro, and McDaniel, *Newsweek* 108, no. 14 (Oct. 6, 1986): 61.

While things can always improve further, and there is always need for ongoing improvement, things have improved a great deal since I was released in 1998. Today, TDCJ credits its Rehabilitation Program Division (RPD) as being primarily responsible for the serious reduction of its recidivism rate—down from 86 percent at the time I was in the system to 21 percent. More than 90 percent of RPD is comprised of chaplaincy services, classes, and programs of many types. A total of more than 23,000 religious volunteers go into Texas prisons year in and year out, preaching, teaching, and pouring into the lives of inmates, and the results speak for themselves. "The Texas recidivism rate remains one of the lowest, if not the lowest, in the nation."[19]

19. *Criminal Justice Connections* 24, no. 3 (Jan/Feb 2017), accessed Dec. 21, 2017, https://www.tdcj.state.tx.us/connections/JanFeb2017/Images/JanFeb2017_agency_lbb.pdf.

CHAPTER IV

LOCKED UP BUT JUSTIFIED BY JESUS CHRIST

> You shall not pervert the justice due to your needy brother in his dispute. Keep far from a false charge, and do not kill the innocent or the righteous, for I will not acquit the guilty.
>
> —Exodus 23:6–7

When I went into prison, I was twenty-two years old and a seventh-grade dropout. I was very angry at the justice system because I was essentially given a life sentence for driving off with someone else's car. I admitted that I was wrong to do that, and I deeply regretted it, but my confession did not change the district attorney's choice to charge and try me for aggravated robbery with a deadly weapon.

I deserved to be punished, but I do not think I deserved the harsh sentence of ninety-nine years in prison that was handed down to me. The aggravated part of the charge was a new instrument designed to strengthen and enhance prison sentences, primarily for repeat offenders, and I was a second-time offender. It was also used as a sentencing utility to pressure offenders into plea bargaining through the threat of more than likely receiving a longer sentence. To this day, the tactic has worked successfully in countless cases. For prosecutors, it's a conviction either way, whether the accused take the deal or not.

I became a victim of the aggravated law because I refused to plead guilty for a crime I did not commit. Consequently, I was sentenced under the aggravated law, which forced me to serve twenty flat years to become eligible for mandatory supervision parole release.

The prison system worked us like slaves, picking and chopping cotton from sun up to sun down in heat up to 116–118 degrees. We picked and bagged potatoes, picked and hauled watermelons, and picked pecans in the fall/ winter season, crawling on our knees through cracking peanuts. All day long, we chopped weeds, cleaned turn rows in the fields, and broke and toted rocks from one place to another. We were worked like slaves and sometimes fed like dogs.

Eventually, the federal courts made the state prison system stop working us in that kind of heat. Because of the court's order, we started working half days—but they decided to take us out to the fields much earlier than the usual work time. We started work at five o'clock in the morning instead of seven o'clock. We still worked very hard all the time through all the seasons of the year. Back then in prison, there was no such thing as having a choice to work or not. Everybody in prison was going to work, or be punished in such ways that it was wiser to just go on to work than suffer the cruel, unusual punishments. The field labor was endless, back-breaking work, day in and day out, year after year. I realized that slavery was not over, only hidden away from public viewing. I worked in the fields for almost four years, but there was a positive outcome. Even though initially it was hard and cruel work, it worked the drugs out of my system and assisted me in developing a good work ethic.

For most of the inmates, the work was hard primarily because they never had a job, and if they did, they did not stay with it for any length of time. The labor was extremely difficult for some men, but in time most came to accept the reality of doing hard slave labor versus suffering the consequences for not working. Some men would collapse from the heat of the sun, trying to keep up with whatever squad they were assigned to. If a man did not keep up with his squad, he was punished in various painful and cruel ways that motivated him to work harder and keep up.

There was a popular saying in the fields, "Get it like you live," which meant "the hard way." In some ways, the work broke a man down, but it broke him in such a way that it gave him a sense of what it meant to work and earn his own things in life. Some men were broken down too far, which ended in demeaning ways that caused them to be raped and brutally emasculated. For others, like me, the work broke us for the good and instilled an appetite to become better men. After I had been worked into better health (when all the drugs had drained out of my system), I felt better than I had in a long time.

One evening, as we came in from the fields, I was sitting in the dayroom waiting to go to my cell when I heard a voice that said, "Get up and go to your cell." I thought I was hearing someone talking to me, so I looked around and asked the few guys sitting next to me if they had said something to me, but they said no. Then I heard the same voice a second time, and this time I got up and asked the guard to let me in my cell, which usually was not going to happen, because normally everyone went into their cells at the same time. This time, it seemed urgent for me, so the guard let me into my cell—much to my surprise.

When I stepped into my cell, I could not see or hear any outside noise—and it is always noisy in prison. During this time, I was out of touch with my surroundings, but I heard a voice saying to me, "My Father calls you. You will preach the gospel for my Father. You will speak for my Father in many places." The voice said to me, "Look," and I began to see myself preaching and talking to people in many places I had never been. I do not know how much time elapsed during this experience, but I knew I was saved by the power of Jesus Christ and that Jesus spoke to me in the cell where I had been living for four years.

When it was over, my cellmate was scared and almost standing up on his bunk. His eyes looked like they would pop out of his head. He said, "Hood, what happened to you?" He went on to say that he could not see me for a while, like something was covering me, but he could not tell what it was. He simply was prevented from seeing me.

He told me after the encounter was over that I looked different and was shining with a glow on my countenance. I told him what I heard and he said he knew it was something like that, but it really scared him.

I was on the floor on my knees with tears streaming down my face. I knew I had experienced the presence of Jesus Christ. I felt like I was brand new. For the first time, I understood what born again truly meant. I still had many years to serve, but somehow at that time it did not matter. The only thing that mattered to me was that I was saved and I knew it! It did not bother me anymore about being in prison because I was free.

I was set free spiritually by the power of Jesus Christ in a prison—in the notorious Eastham prison unit, which at the time was nicknamed "the land of no return." In my case, unlike most, I didn't start to live right because I was eventually released on parole—I started living right long before I got out of prison. I became somebody when I had nothing. I learned to value myself and my life when others said I had no value at all. I began to make a better life for myself when others told me to quit because death would find me before I would get out of prison.

Jesus Christ is the only power with the strength to transform and renew any man into a "new creation." I started to live right because Jesus Christ justified me. He justified me in a prison cell, and I knew I had experienced the transforming power of Jesus Christ. Although I was still suffering the consequences of my prior choices,

I knew I was beginning to heal. Sometimes healing may be a difficult and painful journey, but healing that comes through the Lord Jesus brings with it a joy that is unfathomable, a way of knowing how to suffer for something and the patience to wait on the Lord.

CHAPTER V

DYING TO LIVE

> Education means emancipation. It means light and liberty. It means the uplifting of the soul of man into the glorious light of truth, the light by which men can only be made free.[20]
>
> —Fredrick Douglass

The next morning, I woke up and asked the guard to write me a pass to go to the education department because I wanted to go to school. He laughed at me and walked away. I called him again and asked him again to give me a pass to the education department because I wanted to go to school.

He said to me, "Hood, do you realize that you have to do twenty flat years before you get out of here? You will not make it!" He told me that I would have a stroke or a heart attack, or get shanked (stabbed with a prison-made knife), before I made it out of prison.

I said to him, "You don't know who came to me yesterday evening. You don't know what happened to me yesterday. Write me a pass so I can go to school to begin getting ready to preach and speak for the Good Lord."

20. Frederick Douglass, *The Essential Douglass: Selected Writings and Speeches* (Indianapolis: Hackett Publishing, 2016), 355.

That's what Jesus had told me to do, but I realized I was a dummy with barely a seventh-grade education, and I was not ready to preach or speak to anyone. Most of my vocabulary consisted of four-letter words.

The guard wrote me a pass but still laughed at me. When I got to the education office, I asked to enroll in GED classes, and they too started laughing at me. They also said to me, "Hood, you've got to do twenty years flat, and do you know where you are? This is the Ham, man—Eastham!" Located in Lovelady, Texas, the Eastham unit—nicknamed "The Ham"—at the time I was there was considered the worst and most dangerous prison in the state of Texas. In fact, Eastham was featured on the cover of *Newsweek* on October 6, 1986, with the article titled "Inside America's Toughest Prison,"[21] and it was discussed at length in Robert Perkinson's 2010 book, *Texas Tough: The Rise of America's Prison Empire.*[22]

Even so, the clerks enrolled me in a weekly GED class in 1979. I attended faithfully until I completed my GED preparation, then took the test and got my GED in 1981. After that, I started attending Lee Junior College, a two-year degree program offered at Eastham. I earned my first college degree in 1984, an Associate of Arts in Science, all the while incarcerated at the worst prison in the

---

21. Reported by Daniel Pedersen, Daniel Shapiro, and Ann McDaniel, *Newsweek* 108, no. 14 (Oct. 6, 1986): 46–61.
22. Perkinson, *Texas Tough*, 42–46, et al. Eastham is mentioned on a total of 26 pages.

state of Texas—the worst in the entire nation, according to *Newsweek.*

After earning my first AS degree, I continued my education at Lee Junior College, earning a second AS degree in 1987. Even though I was still in prison, attending college and learning began to change my life. I witnessed myself learning to comprehend things better. I began to communicate better, and I began to see myself doing better and living better. Education can change a man's perspective about himself and the society in which he lives. It will correct his understanding and compel him to understand that he and his choices connect him to his community. Education will inform a man of the crime of ignorance.

I began to envision myself with a good life, a good career, and a good wife. These were not just dreams, they were specific goals and aspirations. I could almost taste it, and when I pictured the future, I saw myself being invited to functions, as I had never been in my entire life. Who would invite an old crook like me to nice evenings of fun and casual socializing? What wild thoughts I had about who I wanted to be and what I wanted to accomplish! Still, I dared myself to dream. I pushed myself hard, and I could see tangible and regular progress, which inspired me to work that much harder.

To this day, I believe it is necessary to see your life before you can live the life you want to live. Dare yourself to dream, and to dream large, and then chase your dreams until they start chasing you and become your realities. I read an article once by Rev. Jessie Jackson, who said, "If you can conceive it and believe it, you can achieve it." I believed that statement, and I lived that statement, as evidenced throughout my life. I was told many times during my incarceration that I would not make it out of prison—and several times a hit was put out on my life (an order to kill me). But by the grace and mercy of the Lord Jesus, I am still on top of the ground, and the ground is not on top of me!

I was relieved from field work and began working in the kitchen, first as a baker and finally as a bookkeeper. I really did not want to work there at first, but one of the guards began talking to me about the Lord and the scriptures. That got my attention, and I began to look forward to the conversations. These talks about God and the Bible reminded me of the discussions—lectures would be more accurate—that my grandfather had had with me. As I recalled those times listening to my grandfather, I began to realize what had caused the disconnect with my family and my community—and most of all from myself and my true identity. I began to discover the issues that had started me on the path toward becoming lost. I began to unravel the estranged feelings between me and my sister. I began to see that she did not realize what she was doing to me, and I forgave her. Despite so many years in prison, I began to realize that I was not dead.

I was *dying to live* in the resurrected Jesus Christ whom I had always known, at least in part. Even as a schoolboy,

I was a Bible boy first. I was lonely for my relationship with Christ. I was hungry for the reading and teachings of the holy scriptures that my grandfather had taught me. When my sister and her husband brought my baby sister and me back to Houston, all those years ago, they never spent time with me reading the scriptures. They did not have any long discussions with me about Matthew, Mark, Luke, and John.

I understood that God was using a prison guard in place of my grandfather to speak to me once again. To this day, that prison employee and I are good friends, and we talk, visit, and worship with each other on a regular basis. Praise God in Jesus Christ who blessed me to rediscover my life and my identity in a prison. I may have been locked up, but God was not locked out.

It has been said that to recover oneself, something must die. This is also reflected in scripture, which notes that a seed must die to produce the plant embedded within its DNA (1 Corinthians 15:36). In my case, I needed to die to my old self, my old life, and my old identity, to be reborn as a new person, with a new life and a new identity in Christ. Simultaneously, I was dying to live, and I was dying to self, which was giving me new life. The passage in 2 Corinthians 5:17 captures this well: "Therefore, if anyone is in Christ, he is a new creation; the old has passed away, behold, the new has come."

CHAPTER VI

SAVED AND SANCTIFIED BY THE BLOOD OF JESUS CHRIST

Don't Quit

When things go wrong as they sometimes will, when the road you are trudging seems all up, when the funds are low and the debts are high, when care is pressing you down a bit, rest if you must but don't you quit.

Life is queer with its twists and turns, as everyone of us sometimes learns, and many a failure turns about, when he might have won had he stuck it out; don't give up though the pace seems slow, you may succeed with another blow.

Success is failure turned inside out—the silver tint of the clouds of doubt, and you can tell how close you are, it may be near when it seems so far; so stick to the fight when you're hardest hit—it's when things seem worst that you must not quit.

—Unknown Author

The above poem was given to me when I was incarcerated, and I leaned on it many times for inspiration. For a little while, attending college became a problem for me.

Many inmates resent a fellow inmate who tries to improve themselves beyond their environment. They do not like seeing another inmate going to school, and especially college, and they are even more resentful if that inmate attends school or college consistently. But also, after a while, when an inmate changes his behavior, the prison staff might take notice of him and the things with which he occupies himself. They will begin to show the inmate some respect and human decency when they realize he is serious about college and changing his life. I made it known that I would change my life for the good, and it was clear that I did not want to live like a caged animal with the label of convict.

Something proud inside of me was bigger and stronger than I was, which compelled, pushed, and stretched me to find myself and get to know just who and what I really was. I wrote to universities, religious orders, college philosophy departments, and even monasteries asking for any books, any literature that they would have discarded and could send me for study. I told those to whom I wrote that I was in prison, and I was trying to figure out how I lost my way in an effort to recapture my life. I was desperately in search of answers about life. The people to whom I wrote responded with books and more books from all over the world—Europe, Great Britain, Denmark, even Tibet, from which country Tibetan lamas wrote encouraging notes to me inside of some of the books they sent.

I had books under my bunk and underneath two other inmates' bunks, whom I paid in commissary for storage fees. I worked during the day, and read books and studied most of the night until breakfast chow time, which began at 3:45 a.m. When morning chow began, I would sleep until it was time to go to work. This became my schedule and routine for nearly fifteen years.

I became a target of resentment and hate because I chose to educate myself. Two hits were put on me with the intent to take me out. One took place in my cell early one morning by sneak attack, at about 2:30 a.m. An acquaintance of mine had informed me about it the evening before, that they would send a couple of guys to do it. I waited, very frightened and scared, and finally, as I lay down to wait (not sleep), four inmates walked into my cell. All four had shanks, and I stood up to meet them. I was angry because they wanted to hurt me for trying to improve my life and myself.

I asked them what took them so long. I told them that I had been waiting for them all night, and that I was glad they finally made it. I said to them that I was happy they had come, because the sentence I had was too much time to do, so they would help me get past it.

"Come on and do the job you all came to do, bring it on," I said. I told them I would be mad if they could not do the job they came to do. I was really scared and trembling on the inside, but they could not see that. I was really talking trash and talking "big six" (six feet under) even though there were four of them. I was talking out of my mind, which probably made them think that I didn't care about what they came to do. I knew they were not scared in any way, and I knew one of them from the streets of Houston, and he knew me. Hate and resentment can cause a man to lose his human decency while in situations like that—they can cause a man to become temporarily insane.

Finally, one of the guys said, "Hood, you know I don't like you, and especially since you think you are better than us because you are getting some education. Just because these officers and wardens are hollering [speaking] at you in the halls doesn't make you any better than us."

I told him, "I don't like you either, so let's get it on."

He stared with deep hostility and said to the other guys, "Let's get out of here." He said, "Hood, I don't know what it is about you but I can't touch you." They turned and walked out of my cell. I sat down all night praying and thanking God for saving me—again.

Sometime after that, those same inmates and I became acquaintances with respect for each other. Other inmates who knew me told me that they dreamed about me, in which dreams I was preaching and speaking in various places. These were places they did not know, but they were sure about what they saw and they believed it was the Lord who showed it to them. They told me that I would do well when I got out of prison.

I continued attending Lee Junior College until there were no more classes for me to take that were provided through their curriculum at the time. At that point, I put in a request to be transferred from the Eastham unit to the Wynne unit in Huntsville, Texas, to begin working on my four-year college degree.

When some of the inmates found out that I would be transferring to Wynne, another attempted hit was put out to kill me before I left the unit. I was walking down the hall early one evening, and one of the turnkeys slammed the gate on my hand and I could not get it out. Several inmates beat me mercilessly. I was left with a broken nose and broken ribs, and my small finger was just about ripped off from hanging in the gate. After the guards finally made them leave me alone, I was loaded into the meat wagon (ambulance) and taken to the primary hospital in Huntsville, Texas, known as the Walls unit.

After my hand, nose, and ribs were patched up, I was returned to my assigned unit. Some of the guys who knew and had some respect for me told me that the guys who attacked me had been taken care of (prison justice).

I was still waiting for my transfer to be approved, which happened about three or four months later. I was transferred to the Wynne unit, where I registered to attend Sam Houston State University. Attending college for a bachelor's degree, I became somewhat like another person. My entire outlook and perspective about life, as well as my view of myself, totally changed. I realized how foolishly I had lived. I regretted the things I had done, and

I felt ashamed of myself. I thanked the Lord that I had never hurt anyone, but I had hurt myself severely.

I studied under some of the finest professors in the state. I earned my bachelor of science at Sam Houston State in 1987, but I continued to attend classes until I was told by the Texas Board of Regents that I could not attend Sam Houston anymore because I had incurred more than 367 class hours of study.

The college did not offer a master's degree at that time, so even with the advice of my professors to continue, the Board of Regents would not allow me to take any more classes. They wrote to me stating that they "saw no need" for me to continue college. They had classified me as a "professional scholar." I asked my professors and the wardens to call some of the board members on my behalf, which they did, but to no avail. They commended me on my scholastic achievements but would not allow me back in college. I wondered if their decision was compelled by the grants being exhausted that had allowed me to attend college. It made sense to me that if I kept my GPA up, I should be able to continue to attend classes. It seemed to me like a good choice since I had such a long sentence. I even wrote them myself because I was lonely and missed school. Imagine that—a seventh-grade dropout, lonely for school!

A Tribute to My Heroes

> [Lee College] employees meet the higher education needs of inmates on a contractual basis on seven units of the Central Region of the Texas Department of Criminal Justice and one private prison in Cleveland, Texas. Student enrollment averages about 1,000 students per semester. To enroll, offender students must meet all academic requirements of the college and the state, in addition to security clearance requirements of the Texas Department of Criminal Justice.[23]
>
> —Lee College website

Today, I am sincerely grateful to all the professors who take the time and effort to go into risky prisons to educate men who have been labeled unworthy and dangerous. They are true heroes in my eyes. Several people whom I met during my incarceration have visited the prisons along with my church members and I to share the gospel and worship with the inmates.

I served seven years in hell's roughest, worst prison in the state, "The Ham," after which I served twelve years at the Wynne unit, and finally, I served my last year of incarceration at the Hightower unit in Dayton, Texas. Prison life can be extremely hard, cold, and viciously cruel. Sometimes I would not talk to anyone and asked that others

23. Lee College, "About Lee College Huntsville Center," accessed Jan. 13, 2017, http://www.lee.edu/lchc/about-lchc/.

would not to talk to me. I was deeply broken and endlessly tried to fathom how a man could get a prison sentence of ninety-nine years for an eleven-minute joyride, while other men sometimes got only five years for murder and other crimes much worse than grand theft. I was bitterly angry, and there was no one with any compassion to talk with me, or to at least listen to me vent.

Then one day God brought another guard into my life who showed me genuine compassion and understanding. He was the new captain over the kitchen where I worked as one of the bookkeepers, after the previous captain retired. He began talking to me about my life and told me I still had a chance to make something of my life. He told me that he did something prison guards were not supposed to do, which was to read the reason an inmate was in prison. He told me that he had read my card, after which he told the warden that I should not be locked up, especially with the sentence I had. He told me the courts really dealt me a cold, bad hand.

The warden agreed with him and shared with him that the front staff also had discussed my case. They agreed that I should not have been sent to prison for the offense I committed. For the first time in many years, someone who worked in the criminal justice system told me they were sorry for what the system had done to me.

The warden told me personally that it was wrong for the court to give me such a harsh sentence. Those words brought me a much-needed sense of comfort and pride.

That was the time in my life when I decided to try to smile again. That was the day when I began to believe that I had some self-worth. That was the day when I started dying to live, because I realized that if I was going to live a better life, the old Marvin had to die. There was a better Marvin inside of me. My grandfather could see that Marvin, and now he had spoken again through a prison guard. He knew he needed to get me somewhere sitting down long enough to hear and listen to him once again—just once more. He knew.

At the time, I still had a long road ahead of me before I would begin to see any hope of getting out of prison. I continued working as a bookkeeper and stayed busy reading and studying my Bible. As time went on, a group of the guys occasionally would gather, and I would teach life skills and the need for education. Most of them enjoyed the discussions, but only a few would attend school or try to attend college after getting their GED. I unsuccessfully tried to teach them that they had to attend classes long enough to acquire discipline in their lives. The men who knew me before my incarceration told me that I had changed; they could tell most of all because I did not talk the way I used to, as my conversation was no longer laced with profanity.

These statements made me feel good. What I had experienced inside was now also visible on the outside. Even so, I had one more blowout to get over. After I had been locked up for seventeen years, I walked into the dormitory where I lived, and I found that an officer had been in my bunk (living area) and had torn it apart. My bunk sheets were on the floor with his shoeprints on them. My books were thrown all over the floor, and the contents of my locker were also thrown on the floor. I blew up and went after the officer who had done it. When I approached him and said I wanted to speak with him, he laughed and told me to get out of his face. I told him okay, but that he would be the one leaving. Later, he was reassigned to another post.

There are things that I am not proud of from during my incarceration. There are things that happened in my life from which I know God rescued and saved me. I have repented and asked for Christ's forgiveness for everything. I believe he has forgiven me and that is all that really matters—Christ paid the price for my sins.

I dedicated my life to serve God while I was still in prison. I asked God to save me, and I made a promise to him that if he saved me I would serve him. I've always remembered that my mother told me I was born to preach for God. Sometimes I think this was what Satan was using other people to prevent me from doing. Maybe, just maybe, they did not realize what they were doing—but neither did I at the time. Regardless, God did know everything about me, which is why he sent his one and only Son to save me. I also never forgot that Jesus Christ told me: "You will preach for my Father!"

When I got out of prison, I went to visit my parents' graves in Marshall, Texas, where they were buried next to each other. I sat at their graves and told them where I had been and asked for their forgiveness. I told them I was ashamed of myself. I sat there for some time, and then I heard my mother say, "Now go and preach." She said, "I love you, Marvin; I had you for God."

I said, "I love you, mother, and I am doing what you told me to do."

CHAPTER VII

FREEDOM FROM PRISON . . . VS. FREEDOM IN CHRIST

Mercy came running like a prisoner set free
Past all my failures to the point of my need
When the sin that I carried was all I could see
And when I could not reach mercy
Mercy came running to me.

—Craig and Dean Phillips, "Mercy Came Running"

Jesus Christ came into my life and saved me right where I was, in prison. There are numerous other men and women whose past mistakes and bad choices end up leading them to the streets or prison. They need to hear that their past mistakes can serve as a positive resource that can propel them into a better life. They need to hear and realize that what they used to do, where they used to go, and how they used to live cannot cancel out their entire future.

They need to know that Christ is looking for them, and they need to be on the lookout for him. No matter what others say about them, they need to know that Christ has forgiveness to offer them. They need to know that Christ loves them despite what they have done. They need to know that Christ will hire them when others won't. They need to know that a new life is waiting for them in Christ. Following scripture's calling, we as Christians must become available to tell them about the new life that awaits them (Galatians 6:1). They do not need to be singled out as former inmates in any kind of church context, during family dinner night, or at any other social occasion. They need to be called and respected by their maternal/fraternal family-given names—not former offender or ex-convict, which retains a connotation of worthless and useless for many. There are better names that are better suited for a new and better person. What about saved, believer, or brother? Or simply calling the person by their rightful name?

Parole—A Second Incarceration

> [Probationers and parolees] are subject to regular surveillance and monitoring by the police and may be stopped and searched (with or without their consent) for any reason or no reason at all. As a result, they are far more likely to be arrested (again) than those whose behavior is not subject to constant scrutiny by law enforcement. [They] are at increased risk of arrest because their lives are governed by additional rules that do not apply to everyone else. Myriad restrictions on their travel and behavior (such as a prohibition on associating with other felons), as well as various requirements of probation and parole (such as paying fines and meeting with probation officers), create opportunities for arrest.[24]
>
> —Michelle Alexander, *The New Jim Crow*

24. Alexander, *The New Jim Crow*, 93.

Freed prisoners are hurting to be respected and craving to be allowed to earn a good living and conduct a good, clean, moral life in peace. They are hurting and grieved to be constantly considered as a non-citizen. They may or may not be on parole, but they are paying taxes like everyone else—despite a lack of equal representation for them.[25] They, like I did for many years, exist under the societal radar as invisible people because they are on parole or mandatory parole supervision, sometimes for ten or more years. They have been ushered quietly out of mainstream life as useless, unworthy, and insignificant. They are afraid of how people will respond to them and what they will say if they are found out to be on parole or state supervision.

I have stated all along that it is fair and just to punish people for crimes they have committed, but it is also fair to release them at an appropriate time to resume their lives as free people. Extended periods of time on parole or under state supervision in many cases translates to over-incarceration, which is judicially abusive.

Power that uplifts and restores life is healthy and restorative, but power that holds men hostage simply because it can and without proper judicial review is abusive,

25. As stated, in Texas alone more than 70,000 prisoners are released every year—79% of whom will not re-offend, and all of whom will eventually be "off paper" (finished with their parole or probation). Nationwide, this comprises a significant population, most of whom arguably are more determined than the average citizen to appreciate their new life, take their responsibilities seriously, and commit to their jobs and families. Once their civil rights are restored, they are also a significant block of voters deserving to have their concerns heard. Recidivism rate from the TDC publication *Criminal Justice Connections* 24, no. 3 (Jan/Feb 2017), accessed Dec. 21, 2017, https://www.tdcj.state.tx.us/connections/JanFeb2017/Images/JanFeb2017_agency_lbb.pdf.

cruel, and morally inhumane.[26] This type of power is dangerous and insensitive toward human decency, and it erodes the moral worth and dignity of life. It is deeply disturbing and cruel for a man to helplessly watch his life be destroyed a second time—first by his own doing in prison, and then by society once he is supposedly set free. This is done on a mass scale and without any remorse by those who cannot say they are unaware of the suffering that this "second incarceration" inflicts, but who will not or cannot stop because of political ramifications. They cannot allow themselves to become known as a "convict lover" or "criminal sympathizer." That type of rhetoric is potentially damaging to careers, but it is more damaging to those affected who have changed their lives personally and spiritually.

Much of the social unrest, discontent, and breach between law enforcement and communities are the result of people represented in this text. If they don't have personal experience, these are people who either have or had a spouse, sibling, parent, grandparent, child, uncle, aunt,

26. Effective Sept. 1, 2017, Texas did away with solitary confinement as a punishment because it was deemed to be "cruel and unusual punishment," which violates the Eighth Amendment of the Constitution ("No one shall be subjected to torture or to cruel, inhuman, or degrading treatment or punishment"). Yet is it not also "cruel and unusual punishment" to allow excessive parole time post-release, with almost impossible restrictions and hair-trigger violation rules? Should something as easy to incur as a speeding ticket be the reason someone returns to prison for years on end? This is just one example of how society has all but ignored and has collectively grown insensitive to the human rights of ex-offenders who have already served their time for their crime. See Keri Blakinger, *Houston Chronicle* (Sept. 21, 2017), "Texas Prisons Eliminate Use of Solitary Confinement for Punitive Reasons," accessed Dec. 21, 2017, http://www.houstonchronicle.com/news/houston-texas/houston/article/Texas-prisons-eliminate-use-of-solitary-12219437.php.

niece, nephew, cousin, neighbor, or friend directly impacted by the criminal justice system. The anger and hostility that is present comes from a long way down, deep inside the many lives that were once hurt by the criminal justice system or were victims of the criminal justice system somewhere in time.

All along, I have consistently stated with sincerity that I respect the criminal justice system, but not because it almost crushed the life out of me. I respect it because it is necessary and overall better than the system in many nations; but it could be a better system, if not for me, then maybe for others in the future. There is no reason why the criminal justice system could not be an institution nationally recognized for rehabilitating men's and women's lives.[27] Much progress has already been made, which should continue in the same trajectory and not allow for backward steps and the straddling the fence of yesterday's thinking. There is no need for the "old school" mindset of malicious policing in prisons or jails that emanates threats and intimidation rather than concern, safety, trust, protection, and cooperation with those who work

27. The state of Texas, for example, by leading the nation in its low recidivism rate of 21% (down from 86% during my early years of incarceration), has attracted numerous other states still in the 50–60% recidivism bracket who want to know what Texas is doing differently. The answer is RPD—Rehabilitation Program Division—90% of which is comprised of chaplaincy services, classes, and programs of many types. A total of more than 27,000 religious volunteers go into Texas prisons year in and year out, preaching, teaching, and pouring into the lives of inmates, and the results speak for themselves. "The Texas recidivism rate remains one of the lowest, if not the lowest, in the nation." From *Criminal Justice Connections* 24, no. 3 (Jan/Feb 2017), accessed Dec. 21, 2017, https://www.tdcj.state.tx.us/connections/JanFeb2017/Images/JanFeb2017_agency_lbb.pdf.

alongside security toward rehabilitation. When inmates are transformed while inside, they carry that with them upon release, and all of society is better off. What is not to encourage about this? What will it take to change the thinking that simply and perpetually condemns inmates both inside and outside prison?

The same malicious policing that defines some officers inside prison also exists on the streets before people are arrested. There have been too many fatal responses when police thought someone had a weapon of some kind. This is policing based on negative profiling and on cultural traits that are different from those of the officers. The idea that blacks are considered prone to violence and destruction is based on false complaints derived from racial divisiveness. The plain truth is that anyone from any race in any context has the potential to become violent. Yet research shows that a higher percentage per capita of black men versus other races receive longer sentences and are prisoners of parole for longer periods of time.[28] These are men who cannot leave the state without permission, who are rejected outright from many jobs because of their record, who are rejected from many housing options for the same reason, and who live in perpetual fear of the smallest infraction, such as driving through a speed trap, which could put them in front of an aggressive

28. ACLU, "Racial Disparities in Sentencing," (Oct. 27, 2014), accessed Dec. 22, 2017, https://www.aclu.org/sites/default/files/assets/141027_iachr_racial_disparities_aclu_submission_0.pdf.

officer, or missing a weekly parole meeting due to their car breaking down. Does this sound like freedom?

These are people who work and pay taxes but cannot vote, among other severely restricted options. When does freedom come for them? If they behaved well enough to be released from prison, then why are they restrained and held for extended periods of time on parole without any new offenses or violations of supervision?

According to the New York Legal Action Center, the reality of parole has the opposite effect that people tend to assume from the theory:

> More than 630,000 people are released from state and federal prisons every year, a population equal to that of Baltimore or Boston, and hundreds of thousands more leave local jails. Rather than helping them successfully transition from prison to community, many current state and federal laws have the opposite effect, interfering with the rights and obligations of full citizenship in nearly every aspect of people's lives. These laws diminish public safety and undermine the nation's commitment to justice and fairness, creating roadblocks to basic necessities for hundreds of thousands of individuals who are trying to rebuild their lives, support their families, and become productive members of communities.[29]

29. Legal Action Center, "After Prison: Roadblocks to Reentry," accessed Jan. 5, 2018, www.lac.org/roadblocks.html, 8

Parole Realities

- Most states allow employers to deny jobs to people who were arrested but never convicted of a crime.
- Most states allow employers to deny jobs to anyone with a criminal record, regardless of how long ago or of the individual's work history and personal circumstances.
- Most states ban some or all people with drug felony convictions from being eligible for federally funded public assistance and food stamps.
- Most states make criminal history information accessible to the general public through the internet, making it extremely easy for employers and others to discriminate against people on the basis of old or minor convictions, for example to deny employment or housing.
- Many public housing authorities deny eligibility for federally assisted housing based on an arrest that never led to a conviction.
- All but two states restrict the right to vote in some way for people with criminal convictions.[30]

Where Do We Go from Here?

> The longer a prison corporation holds an inmate, the more money the company makes. The worse they do the job of reforming the inmate, the more likely the prisoner will continue to recidivate and produce future profits for the company.[31]
>
> —Joel Dyer, *The Perpetual Prisoner Machine*

While humane treatment of prisoners has significantly improved over time, mostly due to class action lawsuits

30. "After Prison: Roadblocks to Reentry," 8.
31. Dyer, *The Perpetual Prisoner Machine*, 275.

such as the 1980 Ruiz v. Estelle case in Texas,[32] the entrenched parole system is as archaic as chain gang labor, and it is long due for a systemic review and overhaul.

The question being asked amid the current crisis of social discontent regarding community policing standards is, "Where do we go from here?" As I consider the oppression and suppression that men and women have endured under the criminal justice system, and those men and women who are further subjected to the scrutiny of the same system throughout their parole, I strongly suggest that as a society, we are probably going nowhere fast as far as changing the current crisis. This is because of the thousands of men and women who entered the system that was supposed to offer them a chance to correct their lives, but instead mistreated them simply because it could. The system took advantage of their free labor without any positive regard for their human worth. I am happy to learn about the giant steps of progress that have been made in the last several decades, but much reform remains to be done to create a true system of rehabilitation and restorative justice compared to simple punishment of criminals. A healthy and robust balance is needed between just punishment and proven methods of rehabilitation. Even more importantly, when the business of

32. This pivotal case, which started as a hand-written petition, resulted in major changes in policies about how prisoners were treated in Texas, including overcrowding, lack of access to health care, and abusive security practices, which were proven to violate the Constitution's Eighth Amendment protection against "cruel and unusual punishment" afforded to all US citizens. From "Ruiz v. Estelle," Wikipedia, accessed Dec. 19, 2017, https://en.wikipedia.org/wiki/Ruiz_v._Estelle.

running prisons is essential to a state's economy, then we have lost sight of the original purpose of punishment, and rehabilitation tragically takes a backseat to profits.

I speak not only as a former inmate for twenty years, but also as someone who is actively involved in prison ministry, chaplaincy, and restorative justice policies designed to enhance more social and civil approaches toward reducing crime and prison recidivism. I started out writing my thoughts and observations about the current crisis we are facing regarding the disconnect and lack of trust between law enforcement, criminal justice issues, and our communities at large. After forty years, my conclusion is that a serious inquiry is needed to examine the practices and procedural applications of enforcement, justice issues, and parole policies, but it needs to be done through the lens of rehabilitation, in which giant strides have already been made. Negative dialogues, harsh critiques, and especially violent protests, such as have been seen recently in several cities, will not award either prisoners or society any better results toward rehabilitation or change for any of the involved agencies.

I want to applaud and not minimize all the hard work and effective strategies that have been conducted for the past forty years regarding law enforcement, criminal justice issues, and parole policies. I believe that starting with a positive assessment is the key to reevaluating the governing policies and procedural laws, and that the significant progress that has been made needs to be celebrated.

With such a renewed reorientation, decision makers can then readdress the implementation and advancement of more transparency, true sentencing equity, equality in administrative justice, just application of procedural policies, etc. I sincerely believe this is the right path toward a more restorative- and transformative-oriented justice system. Such positive goals will simultaneously energize a renewed effort toward a more just and fair penal system. Building on proven positive progress through regular honest assessments will improve prisoner character, enhance law enforcement's image, and increase the moral aspect of justice. All of this will change the trajectory of prison and parole toward rehabilitation and away from a simple retributive dispensation of the law—especially when economics has clouded all facets of human justice.

What many are learning today about the criminal justice system is not new. The same issues that were prevalent forty years ago were worse then and have been greatly reduced, but shades of the same issues still exist today. Many of the problems that justice watch organizations and teams of legal experts were trying to bring to the attention of the public then have been successfully adjudicated, yet the shadows of the past are still present in the system today. Prison as I knew it a long time ago has changed dramatically, and many good and positive changes have been made, but that does not mean that nothing further needs to be done.

Gleaning Good from the Past

He who opens a school door closes a prison.[33]

—Victor Hugo

It may come as a surprise to learn that I think some of the older strategies should be reinstated because they were effective and more rewarding in the areas of personal development. These disciplines helped to develop healthy respect for the ethics of work, self-discipline, personal contentment, and behavioral and character modification. The critical difference is that they function well when they do *not* include brutality. When administered in a humane way, positive results follow policies such as having a choice to work or not work, attending a GED class weekly, attending self-improvement classes, grading inmate work performance and attitude assessment, etc. These were good individual and personal measurements that helped prisoners to mature and become better people.

I am not suggesting that the system return to past conduct of mistreatment of inmates, but the results mentioned above of character enhancement and a strong moral sense within are good virtues regardless of where they are learned. People sentenced to prison are mostly those who broke the law and should pay for the crime(s) they committed. A large percentage of them are school dropouts, drug abusers with aberrant behavior, and

33. AZ Quotes, "Victor Hugo Quotes about Education," accessed Dec. 24, 2017, http://www.azquotes.com/author/7021-Victor_Hugo/tag/education.

those with attitude issues that need correction. These are issues that are exacerbated with abusive rehabilitation, but improved when that same rehabilitation is humanely administered.

Before 1989, the Texas prison system was referred to as the Texas Department of Corrections (TDC). It was an appropriate name for what it stood for and functionally carried out in the lives of men and women who needed to make corrections. The system was difficult, but it had clear and meaningful objectives for reforming lawbreakers to be better people. It attempted to do exactly what the name said—corrections. Through the years, however, the prison system did less correcting and more warehousing in the name of safety, returning a less improved, less rehabilitated person with little insight or understanding about life. Research shows that state and national governments spend more on prisons and incarceration than on education.[34] In other words, it costs more to incarcerate a person than to educate them, even though it is incomparably less effective.

TDC was a system designed to build a healthy work ethic, educate, provide self-improvement programs, and build self-respect, all of which are fundamental principles of personal correction. These ideas could and would

---

34. Kathryn Hanson and Deborah Stipek, "Schools v. Prisons: Education's the Way to Cut Prison Population," (May 16, 2014), accessed Dec. 22, 2017, https://ed.stanford.edu/in-the-media/schools-v-prisons-educations-way-cut-prison-population-op-ed-deborah-stipek. See also Steven Hawkins, "Education vs. Incarceration," (Dec. 6, 2010), accessed Dec. 22, 2017, http://prospect.org/article/education-vs-incarceration.

transform and mature a young boy or girl into a grown man or woman. Prison life is not easy, and especially in the past had some extremely bad aspects. Prison used to be mean and cruel, and fighting was as normal as working. Gambling was always present, and both drugs and liquor found their way into the system. Yet prisons themselves are just buildings, and what happens inside is determined by the men who live there and work there. There were (and are) some extremely mean and vicious inmates, and some guards fit the same description. At the same time, though, there were just as many good inmates and good guards. My point is that the founding principles—correcting behavior—can still be brought forward to the present, minus the inhumane aspects, and both inmates and society will be better off.

I realize that there are thousands of books addressing the timeless issues of incarceration and rehabilitation. The way I see it, some of the primary contributors to the problems at hand are the veins of racism, hate, and resentment that have penetrated the core and soul of the American social fabric. Can we do anything about such major issues? The answer to the question is yes.

The response to the question, however, must be that we are willing to confront the underlying paralysis that plagues and threatens our society at a systemic level. We must become willing to do something about it, as opposed to doing nothing, living in denial, reacting to it with even more violence, etc., or the current crisis simply will never be rectified. The symptoms may fade for a time, but without addressing the underlying causes, they will make a resurgence in time. Gil Scott-Heron, the famous American soul and jazz musician, poet, and author, would refer to this ebb and flow as "The Late Show." What about those who have seen this "show" somewhere before, or many times before? What about us—what about you, dear reader?

When social progress and growth appear to happen in the context of social harmony, it appears that another monster returns from historical struggles. Spilling the same poisonous venom that once caused so much political and social unrest that it turned into the American Civil War, this monster appears to never sleep; even worse, it never dies. The causes of racism and hate may seem illusive, but my new faith taught me that they are rooted in the one common denominator of all mankind, which is human sin ("all have sinned," Romans 3:23; 5:12). Some sins seem more insidious than others, though, and this clever sin of racism knows how to hide and mask itself behind veneers of kindness and sympathy, but what comes out of its mouth cannot be trusted.

You are of your father the devil, and you want the desires of your father. He was a murderer from the beginning, and does not stand in the truth because there is no truth in him. Whenever he speaks a lie, he speaks from his own nature, for he is a liar and the father of lies.

—JOHN 8:44

The Ultimate Rehabilitation

There stands the cost,
like a veil that has been lifted, now I see.
The gift of what the Father has for me,
beyond the splendor is the vision of the cross
and the Father calls to me,
there stands the cost.[35]

—Larnelle Harris

I do not consider myself an authority with all the right answers to explain the critical and unfortunate crisis we face today in our society. What I do know is that I am saddened and hurt to witness the state of our collective social, political, and spiritual being. As I consider the volatility of the issues and the rumbling undercurrents that threaten our society and peace, I am compelled to respond, because my spirit and conscience are grieved by the troubles that continue to fray and tear the fabric of our social and moral caliber with mounting speed. As Job put it, "I was not in safety, neither had I rest, neither was I quiet; yet trouble came" (Job 3:26, KJV).

It is unsettling and shameful that our humanity and social fabric have become so agitated and critically destructive toward our own wellbeing and destiny. I understand why Jeremiah asked the question, "Is there no balm in Gilead? Is there no physician here? Why then is there

35. Larnelle Harris, "There Stands the Cost," Larnelle Collector Series, vol. 2, Benson Records, 1988.

no healing for the wound of my people?" (Jeremiah 8:22, NIV). We must seek resolve and solace together, in unity, as one society. I believe the time is now more than ever for us to turn our hearts to Jesus Christ. The time is now for us to cry out and cry out loudly for the hand of Jesus Christ, because our society and humanity are in a great mess. It is only by God's grace and mercy that there are still some good people in the world.

We still have a chance. The hands of some people in leadership capacities are unsteady and too risky to trust. But God has always brought the best out of any mess that men have crafted and engineered. It is not a question of whether he can change hearts on a large scale, but whether he will—and Scripture says he will if we humbly call out to him. We must take responsibility and ask him to help us. We must let the words of the Lord lead and guide us in life as we turn to him on our knees at home and in church on Sunday mornings. Jesus said, "I am the bread of life" (John 6:35). Are we not starving for this life-giving bread? What I see amidst our current crisis compels me to seek refuge in the Lord Jesus Christ, because he is our only chance to recover, recapture, resolve, and become reconciled as a people and as the people of God.

As a society, we have everything we have asked for, including the good and not so good, which includes all the destructive things that we have inflicted on ourselves. We have done all the things we wanted to do, ignoring the consequences, and yet we continue pursuing the things we have always pursued, as if repeating the same choices will somehow not produce more of the same devastating results. In most instances, God has not gotten in our way and prevented us from doing such things, but the things we have done and continue to do repress our relationship with him. It appears that justice, righteousness, goodwill, peace, and good faith among men have all been convicted and thrown in jail for being too humble and pure for their own good. Truth and righteousness appear to be unwelcome guests among many venues.

Regret is a moral principle that informs our higher conscience, while neglect is a gross ignorance with no moral ground or goodwill on which to stand. The choices are as timeless as history, and the consequences are equally predictable. We face the proverbial fork in the road—will we keep doing things the way we've always done them, or will we finally decide to choose God's path? "Choose this day whom you will serve" (Joshua 24:15b).

This chapter started with a comparison of the great difference between freedom from prison and freedom in Christ. Many are set free from prison but are still in bondage—likewise, many have never been to prison, but they live in bondage, held fast by the chains of their addictions, their sins, and their inhumanity to man. I questioned whether parole is real freedom, and I hope to have made the case for the dire need to revisit parole policies with the same humanity and eye on the Eighth Amendment as guided Ruiz v. Estelle and other, similar verdicts.

Ultimately, though, there is no true freedom without Christ, who alone performs the ultimate rehabilitation from the inside out. “So if the Son makes you free, you will be free indeed” (John 8:36).

CHAPTER VIII

REFLECTIONS: LIFE IN MY CONSCIOUS INTERLUDE

> From its inception, the state [Texas] has served as a contentious testing ground for rival styles of penal discipline: corporal punishment versus Christian charity, exploitative field labor versus penitentiary-based confinement, retribution versus rehabilitation.[36]
>
> —Robert Perkinson, *Texas Tough*

While preparing this autobiography, I revisited some of the things that had happened to me and some of the situations I had encountered when I was incarcerated, and I also began to reflect deeply on life after prison. I recalled some of the thoughts I had in my mind in prison regarding life, people, and the world. Many of my thoughts, both during and after prison, had not been appropriately processed with any clarity. As I overviewed my experiences, I began to contemplate life from different perspectives, some good, and some not so good. Being much more educated, I was able to survey my life and better articulate my thoughts.

36. Perkinson, *Texas Tough*, 5.

Good, bad, or otherwise, life is life, whether we understand it or not. Yet we can choose to understand life better, more meaningfully, and choose to see how we are all interconnected, regardless of how we live and participate in it. Life and time are intrinsically woven together, and the vicissitudes of life are constant and unceasing. My education was both illuminating and alarming as I began to realize the bigger picture involved with my personal prison experience. Ultimately, I learned that my harsh and unjust treatment and sentence had been driven by the politics of the day and by various highly polarized national forces at work, wrestling between the two main prison theories of punishment and rehabilitation. As well, America was still heatedly divided by race on the heels of the 1960s Civil Rights movement, and the racial temperature in the south was much different than that of the north. Just like how Abraham Lincoln's Emancipation Proclamation did not end slavery mindsets, so too the new Civil Rights laws did not bring an end to wrong attitudes that were deeply embedded in hearts and minds. Had I been sentenced farther north, I might have not had much of a story at all to tell. But I also might not have encountered my Lord and Savior, Jesus Christ, which is why I have something more to say to the world than just one more tragic story.

A Travesty of Justice

> The devil, people and things being what they are, it is necessary for God to use the hammer, file and furnace in his holy work of preparing a saint for true sainthood. It is doubtful whether God can bless a man greatly until He has hurt him deeply.[37]
>
> —A. W. Tozer

In preparing this autobiography, I thought about the day I was sentenced to ninety-nine years in prison and how that sentence devastated me when the judge handed it down to me. The conviction happened very swiftly. I was arrested early Sunday morning in 1976, and the arresting officers told me I was charged with unauthorized use of a motor vehicle. At the scene of the arrest, a few more police arrived and began shouting at me about a robbery that had taken place off the Gulf Freeway at a Steak and Egg Diner. I told the officers I knew nothing about it, but they insisted that I did. I was taken to the city jail and placed in a hold-over room, alone, for three days. During that time, I did not talk to anyone, and no officers came to talk with me about anything. I knocked on the door repeatedly until I was warned not to knock on the door anymore or I would regret it. I tried to talk with the officers, but they slammed the door in my face and walked away. I slept in that small room for three days, and no one ever talked to me about the charge or anything else. The

37. A. W. Tozer, *The Root of the Righteous* (Chicago: Moody Publishers, 2015), 165.

police would come to the door and throw a sack meal on the floor, or throw it at me, but they would not talk to me. There was no regard for personal hygiene.

After three days, the door opened and a policeman dressed in plain clothes ordered me to step out of the room. He did not say anything else to me except, "Come on!"

He took me to go before the magistrate who read me my rights. Interestingly, the magistrate read the charge and looked at me rather perplexed. He asked the officer, "Are you sure the charge was correct?"

The officer responded, "Yes, your Honor."

The magistrate asked him again if he was sure, and he said yes. He then looked down at me and asked me if I knew what I was charged for.

I told him, "Yes, unauthorized use of a motor vehicle."

The magistrate looked sternly at me and said, "Young man, you are charged with aggravated robbery with a deadly weapon."

I said, "No, sir, unauthorized use of a motor vehicle."

The magistrate looked at the officer and again said to him, "Are you sure this is the right charge?"

The officer said, "Your Honor, I am not the arresting officer. I was asked to bring him over here, get him charged, and get his rights read to him."

The magistrate said to me, "Young man, do you have a family?"

I said, "No."

He said, "I hope you can get someone to help you, because this charge does not look right to me." Then he asked the officer, "Do you know anything about this [case]?"

"No, your Honor."

"Where is the alleged weapon?"

"Judge, I do not know anything about this charge or about him. I am doing the other guys a favor. Since I was walking out of the building getting off work, I was asked to bring him over here and get his rights read to him."

The judge looked at me and said, "Young man, this does not look right to me, and I hope you get a good court-appointed attorney." He looked to be of Asian descent, possibly Chinese. I am not sure what his ethnicity was, but I remember what he said to me and to the officer: "This charge does not look right to me, and there is nothing in this charge that shows any violence or use of a weapon."

The judge read me my rights, and I was taken back to the city police building next door and put back in the same room. Several hours later, I was taken to what was known as the Harris County Rehabilitation Center in Atascocita, Texas.

About two weeks later, I was taken to the dressing room and told that I was going to trial. I said, "No, that can't be right because I have not had a lawyer assigned to my case."

The officer told me, "Tell the judge, but get dressed."

I was taken to court, and the district attorney offered me fifteen years for aggravated robbery with a deadly weapon. I told him that I did not rob anyone and that I was supposed to be charged for unauthorized use of a motor vehicle. He told me he did not care what I thought I was charged for, but that he was charging me with aggravated robbery with a deadly weapon.

I said to him, "But I did not rob anyone."

He said, "I don't care what you did. If you can't take the fifteen years, I promise to throw you away."

I tried to talk to him but he refused to listen to me. He treated me like I was a total nobody, like I was trash.

He walked away from the hold-over cell, then turned back to me and said, "You have five minutes to make up your mind. When I come back in here, all I want to hear is that you will take the fifteen years."

When he came back to the cell, I tried to talk with him, but he only asked me if I was ready to take the fifteen years.

I told him, "No, because I did not rob anybody."

He said, "If you choose a jury trial on me, I promise I will throw your life away, —" (using derogatory language).

I said, "You know this is wrong, that I did not rob that man. I drove off in his car."

He laughed at me and walked away.

About forty-five minutes later, I was assigned a lawyer. I had not talked with him about this case, but I had used him before on a DWI charge (driving while intoxicated). My lawyer told me that because he was on file as having represented me before, the court automatically contacted him and assigned him to my case. He told the judge that he had not reviewed the case, that he knew nothing about it, and that he was unprepared for trial.

The judge told the lawyer, "You have forty minutes to review the case and then we are going to trial."

The district attorney was looking at me, laughing.

My lawyer pleaded with the judge to not proceed with the trial, but the judge said to him, "If you say anything to me again about not being ready, I will charge you with contempt of court."

A jury panel was selected and the trial started at 1:00 p.m. I don't remember what day it was, but I do remember that at the end of that day, I was found guilty of aggravated robbery with a deadly weapon. There were no witnesses except the complainant, who had not been harmed, there was no weapon, and there had been no violence—there was nothing that would support the conviction.

The following week, I was brought back to court and sentenced. I was given ninety-nine years of hard labor "for convicts and convicts only" as stated by the judge as he read the sentence, which phrase I only came to understand much later.

The district attorney walked over to me and opened a can of peanut brittle. He said, "Look at that good candy. It will be a long time before you taste anything like that again. I told you I would throw you away. I told you they [the jury] would believe me and not you." He walked away from me, laughing.

The court bailiff took me back to the hold-over cell. He told me that I had been really done wrong because the entire trial was wrong. He said, "I hope you can get a good lawyer and appeal this case because it was not a robbery at all and definitely not aggravated robbery with a weapon." He added, "That D.A. knows he was wrong. He only wants to make judge."

I could not say anything because I was shocked and basically traumatized to get such a sentence for an eleven-minute joyride. Those eleven minutes became twenty years and sixty-one days of hell for me.

I thought my life was over, and at that time to me it was. I became isolated and did not want to talk to anyone during the initial time following my sentencing. I was shipped off from jail to prison within a month and got off the Blue Bird bus at Eastham prison. Although I concealed my fear as best I could, I was very scared.

I spent many, many days trying to figure out what happened to me and why or how I ended up with so much time for such a petty crime. Though I sought assistance from several civil rights entities, none of them would help me—they said they did not accept criminal cases. Day in and day out, I said to myself over and over, "This can't be right! This can't be real!" I finally accepted that it wasn't right, but it was my new reality. I was very bitter for the first several years of incarceration, and I had very little conversation with anyone except myself.

Life in Hell

> Prison reform is a frightfully big piece of work . . . and it can easily absorb all that all of us are and have and still be unfinished unless the Lord Himself will perform a miracle.[38]
>
> —Minnie Fisher Cunningham

Eventually, I began to read. Soon, I was reading everything I could get my hands on from the library. I mostly read religious materials and philosophy books. I later enlarged my search, writing various universities and Christian organizations, requesting any free books or literature they no longer used. Many of them replied, and I began to accumulate a small library with books stacked up underneath my bunk and around the wall of my cell. The officers told me not to stand the books up against the wall and to keep them under my bunk. Eventually, I had to get permission to stand the books up against the wall because I had so many of them. The officers became angry with me and verbally abused me sometimes with threats of bodily harm. I told them they could go on and beat me, but I would not die ignorant and uneducated.

I worked in the fields all day for the prison, and I read all night for myself. I knew I was intellectually deficient and far behind where I should be at my age, and I was

38. Judith N. McArthur and Harold J. Smith, *Minnie Fisher Cunningham: A Suffragists's Life in Politics* (New York: Oxford University Press, 2003), 121.

determined to catch up and then keep going with no end in sight.

I witnessed men being brutally beaten, raped, and sometimes killed. I saw men murdered by someone sticking a pencil in their ear or by being stabbed. I saw a man's arm being chopped off, and I saw men killed for the smallest things, for virtually nothing (see sidebar). One time, I heard the blood-curdling screams of a man who was being castrated with a tuna can lid.

"The Ham"

While things like this didn't happen only at Eastham, a higher than normal percentage of violence occurred there. According to the 1986 issue of *Newsweek* mentioned earlier, "Between January 1984 and September 1985, 52 prisoners were fatally shivved and mangled throughout the 27-unit system (the size of TDC at the time); six died at Eastham."[39]

Keep in mind, this was just in one two-year period, and those numbers didn't include the 622 who were stabbed but survived during the same timeframe. The new violence was a reaction to the power gap left when the courts ordered the end of 1,500 building "tenders" (inmates who ran the cell blocks instead of guards and who routinely "tuned up"—beat up—other inmates who stepped out of line) and the installment of 1,400 new guards. The new plan for control was a long-delayed response to the late 1970s Ruiz v. Estelle case, which had triggered a new era of prison reform—but one that only slowly filtered down to change daily life in hardcore prisons like Eastham. As directed by the courts, new guards were hired to replace the tenders, but that didn't bring instant change. Instead of building tenders running things, gangs stepped in and took control while the inexperienced guards learned the ropes and tried to implement the changing rules.[40]

39. Pedersen, Shapiro, and McDaniel, *Newsweek* 108, no. 14 (Oct. 6, 1986): 48.
40. Ibid., 53–56.

I became familiar with loneliness and with what human brokenness feels like. I felt the demeaning effects of human degradation, disrespect, and being put away and counted as worthless—I felt what it was like to be considered unfit to live among people and to not be received as human.

I thought that if there was anything that could be called hell, prison was it. I was there, and there are no guests in hell, only permanent residents. I was frightened and became very afraid when some of the inmates threatened to kill me for trying to improve my life and become someone better than a convict. That was the mentality during that period of prison life in the 1970s and 1980s (and I learned soon enough that it was even worse before that time). But in prison, you learned to hide and live with your fears.

Prison was vicious, mean, and probably the worst place for anybody to live. As stated, Eastham was considered the worst prison in the state of Texas (for some, in the whole nation), and there is no reason for me to believe it wasn't. According to Perkinson, there were four infamous prisons vying for the title of "America's toughest prison."[41] Along with the daily violence I witnessed all around me, I was beat up a few times, and I was threatened with rape and murder. I thought a lot about the threats and possibly being killed. It was a very difficult time for me; it was the worst fear I had ever imagined.

41. Perkinson, *Texas Tough*, 152.

I absolutely hated the thought of someone wanting to hurt me just because I wanted to become educated and change my life. But it wasn't only the inmates who resented me for my aspirations and goals. Some of the officers resented me as well, and they would harass me when they could. They resented me even more when I started attending Sam Houston State University in Huntsville. They thought that an inmate should not be allowed the opportunity to get an education with taxpayers' money. I could understand the hate and resistance from the inmates, but it was a new level of malicious resentment from the officers. Sometimes they would come to my bunk area specifically to destroy my class assignments. I was deeply hurt and insulted, but I did not stop attending classes; I did not stop reading, writing, and studying.

When my class assignments were torn up, I would pick up the pieces, put them in an envelope, and take them to the warden and my professors. I taped some of them back together if the torn pages were not too tiny. Sometimes, the officers were reprimanded, but my professors still graded the papers (most of the time a good grade, even if they were in pieces). Some of the inmates told me they would tell the warden or sign as witnesses to what happened.

A Bygone Era Still Alive and Well

> The history of racial caste in the United States would end with the Civil War if the idea of race and racial differences had died when the institution of slavery was put to rest."[42]
>
> —Michelle Alexander

Working in the fields and being intimidated, insulted, and treated with contempt, I realized firsthand what twentieth-century slavery looked and felt like. I experienced the ugly, humiliating, cruel temperament of slavery. I also studied about the institution of slavery, and I concluded that what thrived in the previous century still existed in the current century. Much later, I learned that I wasn't alone in my thinking (see sidebar).

A Yale-educated professor of American studies in Honolulu at the time, Robert Perkinson exhaustively researched his 2010 book *Texas Tough*. He extensively analyzed the historical roots of America's prison system, channeling the bulk of his attention on Texas (which included significant focus on Eastham). Here is an example of his unwavering calling out of the direct connection between the "domestic institution" of pre-Civil War slavery and the founding of the state's prison system:

> All of Texas's principle institutions—its political and legal systems, its economy and cultural mores—rested on a bedrock fracture: exalted liberty secured through systematic debasement. So, too, did the first prison at Huntsville. As in other southern politics that later coalesced into the confederacy, Texas developed criminal justice traditions uniquely suited to

42. Alexander, *The New Jim Crow*, 26.

> the political economy of human bondage. Slavery itself was ultimately swept away by the American Civil War, but its criminal justice institutions endured. As Alexis de Tocqueville once remarked, "the Law may abolish slavery, (but) God alone can obliterate the traces of its existence."[43]

In his chapter titled "Worse than Slavery," Perkinson exposed what is today a little-known loophole in the Thirteenth Amendment, although it was apparently well-known at the time:

> (It was a loophole) which prohibited slavery "except as punishment for crime" . . . Texas and other states took full advantage of this exemption in the postbellum years. Rather than housing convicts in expensive penitentiaries, they hired them out to the highest bidder. This practice, known as "convict leasing," developed into the most corrupt and murderous regime in American history. In the Lone Star State, it reached its apex.[44]

During the time I was in prison, I realized that slavery was not limited to an era gone by. Quite the contrary, it was alive, well, and legal for the penal system. The similarities of punishments, and some of the language spoken during slavery times, were still prevalent in Texas more than one hundred years after the Civil War. I reflected a great deal on this, contemplating about slavery, racism, bigotry, and the validity of hate. I learned a lot about how hurtful some people could be to others simply because of the color of their skin. Even my appetites and aspirations for self-betterment were viewed as insignificant and "rascally." In many ways, I was a modern slave. I have personally felt the foot of that evil force in my life and I have been

---

43. Perkinson, *Texas Tough*, 49.
44. Perkinson, *Texas Tough*, 84–85.

held in the hands of its vicious grip. Indeed, this was in free, emancipated America, and it didn't only happen to a rare person here and there. Many officers considered that type of treatment perfectly acceptable for convicts, and public sentiment provided complicit endorsement through silence and willful ignorance. It isn't uncommon to this day to hear people say that if you break the law, you should be locked up and the key thrown away, or that you should be put on bread and water and left to rot, or why don't they bring back chain gangs—or even more explicitly, maybe slave labor wasn't such a bad idea.

I understood the possibility of getting hurt or killed, but I was determined that I would not be raped. There were inmate innuendos and talking smack (empty talk), but nothing I could not handle myself. Sometimes I was warned by other decent inmates about possible hits on my life being circulated. Looking back, Lee Williams' song "Cooling Water" accurately described both my predicament and the saving grace that rescued me:[45]

> My soul was sinking, in a world of sin
> But grace and mercy, it took me in
> And it felt like, cooling water cooling water, cooling water
> It felt like cooling water cooling water, cooling water
> Cooling water from grandma's well . . .

45. Lee Williams and the Spiritual QC's, "Cooling Water," Soulful Healing album, (Alpharetta GA: Majestic Communications Group, 2006), used with permission.

At some point during my self-reflection/self-awareness stage, I learned something about myself that made me feel terribly sad, which was that I had the capacity to hurt someone, and hurt them badly. I felt a great sorrow to realize this about myself. I am ashamed to admit it, but in prison as it was when I was there, you either had to learn to survive, get taken advantage of, or be killed. I was not going to be taken advantage of—to me, death was better.

Yes, I had committed a crime, but the crime I committed was not the crime for which I went to prison. The crime I committed was to commit a crime while black, poor, and uneducated, especially about the legal system. Today, my whole case probably would have been dismissed. At the time, it was enough for a life sentence—and it easily could have been a death sentence.

Sometimes, such as when a prosecutor is flexing the muscles of a new law designed to bolster his political career as being "tough on crime," one human life is seen as a small price to pay. It was just one more numbered individual sacrificed to the growing hunger of the rising prison empire in America[46]; one more insignificant nobody crushed for the greater good, to appease public fear and to pump up a renewed sense of public safety. The problem is that each of those numbered individuals and insignificant nobodies is a living, breathing human being,

46. From Perkinson, *Texas Tough*, the cover subtitle of which—*The Rise of America's Prison Empire*—is apropos for the primary thrust of the book.

made in the image of God, with an eternal soul, and God loves them no matter how bad they are.

The Long, Slow, Predicted Turnaround

> Prisons not only waste money but waste lives . . . they are doing more to resegregate American society than to safeguard America's streets . . . they helped transform the Great Society into a mean society.[47]
>
> —Robert Perkinson, *Texas Tough*

I was in prison when I began to have a sincere and trusting relationship with Jesus Christ, and I know that he interceded for me and protected me during my incarceration. It wasn't the first time that I drew close to him, because I had a great relationship with Jesus Christ at an earlier time in my youth. Sometimes in life you might be dealt a hand you don't think you deserve, but you either live with it or die with it. I chose to live and trust in Christ. I began to remember what I was told about myself before I met myself. There were people who had told me that specific things would happen to me before I would begin to really live and know what life was about. They were right; we seldom know the angels among us.

I remember my mother telling me I was going to be a preacher, and how I would tell other people that my mother said she had me for God. I remember hearing my

47. Ibid., 11.

mother tell me that even at three years old, which was my age when she died. My grandfather and brothers also told me that I would become a preacher.

Around 1971, I was walking into a club, and before I went in, a guy sitting in a black car called my name as I walked by him. I turned to look at him and he said my name again. I asked him how he knew my name, and he said, "Marvin, I know everything about you." I proceeded to walk away, and he called out to me, saying, "Marvin, I have something to tell you."

"You don't have anything to say to me."

"Yes, I do." He asked me to give him just a few minutes, so I did. I asked him again how he knew my name, and he said, "I know everything about you."

I told him that he did not know anything about me, but when I said that, he began to tell me things about myself that I knew he could not have known. One of the things he told me was that I had just gotten out of jail, and he was right.

I asked how he knew that, and he went on to tell me how old I was, that my sister and brother-in-law had put me out of the house, that I liked to sing and favored Sam Cooke, that I was smart but had dropped out of school, and that I had left home because I was unhappy.

"Marvin, you are just hurt. You are not a bad boy."

"You don't know what you are talking about."

"I know everything about you, Marvin." Indeed, he knew my date of birth, and he knew what my mother used to tell me about being a preacher for God. He asked me, "What did your mother tell you that you were born to do?" He even knew my mother's name.

I asked him if he was a policeman and he said no. After that, he told me that he had come to tell me something. I asked him where he was from, but he never told me.

He went on to say, "Marvin, you are going to prison for a long, long time. You will grow up in prison and you will learn many, many things about yourself and the Lord. You will meet Jesus Christ, and your whole life will change when you see him. You will begin to understand life, and you will begin to live and have a good life."

He told me that I would become a preacher and preach in many places. I asked him how long I would be in prison, and he told me that I would be in prison for a very long time—until my early forties. I was twenty-one years old when he told me that. It was a message I would hear again from my ex-wife's aunt. The man smiled, told me goodbye, and drove away. I never saw him again, but he was right. My first time in prison had been for about three years. The second time, I remained in prison until my early forties, just as the strange man had told me that night in his car in front of a club.

As I said before in chapter 3, the first time I got out of prison, I got married, thinking marriage would steer me straight. I stayed out of prison for a couple of years, but then I went back for the second time. The lady I married was the niece of the lady who managed the apartments where we lived, and she had warned me not to leave my apartment the night I was arrested. Just as she had said to me that Saturday evening as I was coming down the stairs headed out to go clubbing, I never came back home.

She had said, "Marvin, if you don't turn around and go back upstairs into that apartment, you won't make it back." She and the man in the black car had told me the same thing with different words. Both messages were the same—I was destined to go to prison for a very long time, but I would begin to live a good life after prison.

A total of three times I was told about myself before I ever really knew myself. I finally met myself while I was locked up. I began to unravel my messed-up life, but I did not do it by myself. Prayer and talking with the Lord provided me with the light of a better understanding. I began to recall the conversations my grandfather would have with me as a young boy. I think he knew I would need to have a conversation at some point. To this day, I say, "Thank you, Papa."

A Personal Calling

> One often sees a call only in retrospect. This too is God's design. God often reinforces our faith after we trust him, not before.[48]
>
> —Ravi Zacharias

48. AZ Quotes, "Ravi Zacharias," accessed Jan. 5, 2018, http://www.azquotes.com/quotes/topics/faith.html.

One night in my cell, I got on my knees and I asked Jesus Christ to empty me, to turn me upside down and shake all the mess out of me, to shake all the things that were not of him out of me. I asked Christ to do this in my life and he did. I asked him that, once he shook everything out of me, he would show me and tell me what to gather of myself, because I did not want to be the same person I had been when I arrived in prison. I asked the good Lord to save me, and I would do whatever he wanted me to do.

Christ said to me, "Do what your mother told you my Father called you to do." I heard him clearly—there was no mistake; there were no doubts! I heard Jesus Christ speaking to me. It was like being baptized in the Holy Spirit!

He said to me, "My Father calls you to preach for him." I knew it was Jesus Christ who spoke to me. No guessing, no doubts; I knew it was Christ. I had encountered Jesus Christ in the Holy Spirit—and I was in prison.

After that, different men came and shared with me that they had had dreams about me, and that I was going to become a preacher. On one occasion, an inmate was moved over to bunk in my area. At that time, I lived in a dormitory of about one hundred men. The beds were really close together because the prison system was extremely overcrowded, which forced us to sleep very close to each other. Such close quarters tended to generate hostility among the inmates. A friend of mine had gotten into a fight with another inmate who was known to be a bad actor (have a bad reputation), as were his friends. As we entered the shower room early on a Saturday morning, this inmate had run over toward me and my friend who I had gotten to know in jail. He ran over from behind us and stabbed the guy I knew in the ear with a broken, jagged-edged hot sauce bottle. That was the first time I knew blood was hot as it splattered onto me. I saw the inmate and raised my hand to block the striking bottle, which prevented my friend from being stabbed in the neck. The inmate who did the stabbing laid down on the ground to surrender, which was the customary thing to do after an attack, as it communicated no resistance and hopefully kept the attacker from being beaten.

In this case, because it was such a violent attack, a beating was coming for sure, and coming soon. As the attacker was being taken out of the shower room, he looked at me and told me I was next for getting into his business. I stared back at him and told him to bring it.

A few weeks later, his brother moved into my bunk area. I was in the day room when he came into the dorm. He went and put his things away in the locker, and then came to the day room. He walked over to me and said, "Hood, you know I came to take you out."

I didn't say anything and he walked away. This inmate and I lived and slept in bunks next to each other with no more than two feet between us. I don't know how he slept, but I slept very lightly and tried to keep both eyes open.

Situations like this created a permanent syndrome in my psyche that I later learned was called hypervigilance. One doctoral student, writing about emotional scars among inmates (and who later became a prison chaplain), described this phenomenon as an enduring physiological aftereffect of trauma.[49] He wrote the following description:

> Hypervigilance is listed by the APA as a diagnostic criterion (Criterion D4) for Posttraumatic Stress Disorder[50] (PTSD) and falls within their general category of anxiety disorders. Dictionary.com affirms: "the condition of maintaining an abnormal awareness of environmental stimuli; (a) person suffering from PTSD may have hypervigilance (or) heightened startle responses and flashbacks."[51]

After several months passed, I came in from work one day, and the inmate who had come to take me out said to me as I came to my bunk, "Hood, I need to talk to you." I just looked at him, and he said again, "No joke, man. I need to talk to you."

I said, "Go ahead and say what you got to say."

He said, "I had a dream about you last night, and I know it was God who spoke to me. He told me not to harm you or bother you. He told me that you belong to him and that you are one of his preachers."

He continued, while I could do nothing but stare at him. "Then he told me to look, and I turned around and

49. Kevin Hrebik, "Within the Context of Physical Scars, Applying Scripture and Bowen Theory to Help Inmates Understand and Overcome Their Emotional Scars," Doctor of Ministry dissertation (Houston Graduate School of Theology, 2012), 9–10.

50. *Diagnostic and Statistical Manual of Mental Disorders: DSM-IV*, 4th ed. (Washington, D.C.: American Psychiatric Association, 1994), 428.

51. Dictionary.com, "Hypervigilance," accessed Feb. 12, 2011, http://dictionary.reference.com/browse/hypervigilance.

saw you preaching everywhere, in many places." He told me that he had hated me but could not hate me anymore. In fact, he said, "I am a little afraid of you, Hood." He said that he knew it was God who showed him these things, and that it was God who had spoken to him. Thereafter, he and I got along well and even began to associate with each other.

A little while after that, another inmate who moved into the same dorm came and told me of a similar dream he had about the same thing, and I don't think the first guy had told him anything about the dream he had had. There was no reason to believe these experiences weren't genuine—no different than the people who had spoken similar things prior to my incarceration.

I Saw Yesterday's Presence—Reflections on My Release

> Let us all hope that the dark clouds of racial prejudice will soon pass away, and that in some not too distant tomorrow the radiant stars of love and brotherhood will shine over our great nation with all their scintillating beauty.[52]
>
> —Martin Luther King, Jr.

I was released from prison in January 1998 after serving twenty years and sixty-one days of confinement in

52. Martin Luther King, Jr., "Letter from Birmingham Jail," accessed Jan. 15, 2018, http://www.mlkonline.net/quotes.html.

the Texas Department of Criminal Justice. The night before I was released, I could not sleep as my mind raced about the things I wanted and the things I wanted to do. I thought about finally having the things most take totally for granted—a choice of food, sleeping in a real bed, using the toilet alone, turning the lights off and on, etc.

I thought about going somewhere other than inside the prison corridors. There were people I wanted to see, some of whom I wanted to tell that their advice was right, that I had been terribly wrong regarding the way I was living, and I had been warned about the destructive ways I was living but I would not listen. Many, many things were going through my mind the night before I was released from prison. There were some things I wished I could take back, things I deeply regretted. I realized I had to own my life, good or not so good. I needed to own my life, and I asked Jesus Christ to bless me to start again, which he did, giving me the strength and fortitude that I needed. Yesterday, I lived for myself; today, I would live for Christ.

I was released to live at my sister's home where I grew up as a kid, albeit as a troubled kid at the age of about twelve or thirteen. I missed my mother and father who were both deceased. This was the home where I was told I could no longer attend the Baptist church I loved because we were going to become members in the Methodist church. This was the home where I asked my sister and her husband (my guardians) to come and watch me play basketball, but they never would. This is where I realized I was not loved, at least in the way I thought love should look. Maybe they did love me, but in ways I did not understand, such as giving me somewhere to live, food to eat, and clothes to wear. Maybe those were provisions that they considered conveyed the love I needed.

I returned apprehensively to the home I grew up in because I had no other place to go. The first couple of weeks went by in an excitingly pleasant way. Each morning, my sister, her husband, and I would drink coffee and get caught up on things from my long absence in prison. I was deeply happy to be free, and I was especially looking forward to establishing a good life for myself, but I had realized during my incarceration that that home was the place that had created and contributed to my troubled life. I had grown up in that house, but that house had been mean and cruel toward me, and my family had hurt me deeply.

I knew this was a challenge that I needed to face to better understand my reasoning about the trouble in my life. Had my troubles really started there? I needed to revisit my thinking, then clarify my thoughts. I needed to verify whether my thoughts had been true or not. I needed to reevaluate whether this really was the origin of my rebellious behavior and my personal and social disaster. I had run from life too many times, moving from house to house, motel to motel, and from one friend's house to another. I had been on the run most of my life, but during my incarceration I decided that I was tired of running. I decided that I would not run anymore, that I would return home, if only to face the demons that struck me down in my own home as a kid. I needed to know the truth, and hopefully I would then understand why.

After I was at home for about four months, my sister's husband became displeased, and his attitude toward me from when I was a kid began to surface again. He had been my nemesis most of my life, just as he had been trouble for my other siblings, but they were not as vocal as I was about it. He began by calling me unwholesome, disrespectful names such as convict and criminal, saying things like, "You'll be back on drugs in a month, convict. The only reason I let you come back here is because your sister begged me to let you come back."

I had an extremely difficult time getting a job because of my incarceration and conviction. There were a few employers who initially considered hiring me, but they simply did not believe I had been in prison for twenty years for unauthorized use of a motor vehicle. Most potential employers thought that I must have killed someone or something equally depraved. A few employers told me flat out that no one goes to prison for twenty years for a car, and I could not convince them otherwise.

Finally, after eleven months and eighteen days, I got my first job at an asbestos company working in the tool room, handing out tools. I was mistreated and the job only lasted about six or seven months. I was the minority at the job and the supervisors wanted to hire someone else in the position instead of me. The supervisors at the site did not hire me; I was hired by the contractor to whom the work was contracted.

Shortly after this, I met an acquaintance of my employer while I was attending volunteer training for prison ministry. I shared with him how difficult it was for me to get a job, and he assisted me in getting a new job through a friend of his. I was paid $7.25 an hour on a weekly basis, which amounted to about $274.00 a week.

After I received my first pay check, my sister told me that I would have to pay rent each week, which was $80. I agreed because I realized that paying my own way was a moral good, but I also wanted them to realize that I was trying to start my life again. They did not feel that way, so I paid the $80 weekly. My brother-in-law initially took me to work, but after the first time giving me a ride, he told me that I would have to pay him $25 a week in gas for the daily trip. Initially, I agreed to it because I had not yet learned how to ride the bus at that point of my release. So, my rent plus gas money totaled $105 per week, which left me $169 per week for everything else—clothes, shoes, lunch meals, hygiene items, etc.

As I began to consider my funds and how to best maximize the money I had, I told my brother-in-law that I would start riding the bus to work, which turned into an argument during a time when he came to pick me up from work. When I told him that I would start taking the bus the next week, he said to me that he should pull the car over and put me out on the road. I asked him not to, and he told me not to say anything else to him, just be glad he would take me home.

Thereafter, there was always tension and arguments between us and verbal abuse toward me. I asked my sister to speak with him about it, but she told me it was his house. I asked her a few more times, but she would not say anything on my behalf. The tensions escalated, but I kept quiet during the attacks, and I would leave if I could get a friend to come and pick me up and take me anywhere but there for a little while.

Then I began to reflect over my past life, and I began reading "Third Isaiah" (Isaiah chapters 56–66) in the Bible, which is referred to as the repentant part of the book. I mention that detail here to share with you how the Lord led me to understand this text as it related to my life experiences. Sometimes, I believe the Lord will heal one in brokenness, and then send him or her back to brokenness to become his witness, sharing critical ideas as lessons learned to assist others in their spiritual growth.

I don't think either my sister or brother-in-law gave their treatment of me a second thought—they were only interested in getting payments out of me any way they could. In my earlier years growing up at home in the same environment, I would run away when things became too intense to handle. This time, I decided that crying out to God was better than running. The Holy Spirit revealed to me that I was not crying out only for me, but for them even more than myself.

I loved my family, even though I knew they did not love me, not even when I was a child. I was merely a social security payment for them and nothing more. Thus, I came face to face with the truths of my destruction. This reminded me of a song I clung to several years ago by Gil-Scott Herron, "Home Is Where the Hatred Is," which includes the line, "Home is filled with pain, and it might not be such a bad idea if I never go home again."[53]

After too much mistreatment on the job, I found myself standing outside on the loading dock at my job, crying out and asking God what to do. I heard the Spirit of the Lord speak to me and say, "I gave you a job a long time ago, now do it." The Spirit said to me, "I called you into ministry to serve me." I called my sister from work and I told her that I was coming home but I was quitting that job. I assured her that I would continue paying my rent because I had saved some money that they did not know about. She said okay, as long as I had rent money.

I left that job, cleaned up an old typewriter my sister had, and I wrote a letter informing the local churches that I had been in prison, and I would like to come to their church and share my testimony with their congregation. I bought some stamps, mailed the letters to several churches, and within about two weeks, I had several invitations

53. Gil-Scott Herron, "Home is Where the Hatred Is," from *Pieces of a Man* album (Ace Records, 1971).

to tell my story about how Jesus Christ came into my prison cell and saved me from hell and myself!

Within a few months, I announced my candidacy for ministry into the United Methodist Church. A meeting was arranged for me with the district superintendent, who visited with me on three occasions. We visited and talked about ministry, my past troubled life, and why I wanted to go into the ministry. After the third visit, he looked at me and said, "Marvin, I am going to do something I have never done. I am going to recommend you to the Bishop for ministry." He added, "I see something in you I have never seen before in someone's eyes." That was a very happy day for me!

Thus, I started my ministry studies and training, until finally, about two or three years later, it was time to go before the Board of Ordained Ministry (BOM). I actually tried to back out of meeting with the BOM because I was afraid of being rejected. The chair asked me to trust in God and trust the process. I told him I would, and sure enough, I was accepted into the Texas Annual Conference of the United Methodist Church. I was shaking in my shoes all the way there. In the meantime, I had gotten married to my beautiful wife, Bonita, who was very supportive of me and very happy when I called her and told her I made it—the BOM!

In retrospect, while living at my sister's home I shared my appetite to go into ministry with my siblings. I shared most of my ambitions with my siblings because I thought they would be supportive and happy for me, but they were not. My ambitions were quickly soured by them telling me that I would not be accepted because I was a convict and that no one would trust me. Actually, my family rejected every idea, dream, or aspiration that I shared with them. Consistently, they told me to just forget the things I wanted to aspire to because I was a convict. My siblings told me to just find a job and try to keep it, because the things I wanted to do were simply out of reach for me. When I first met Bonita, my wife today, I was told I was not good enough for her, and that she would not want anybody like me because I didn't have anything to offer her. I'm happy to say that at the time of writing, Bonita and I have been happily married for twenty years!

My family were not the only ones attempting to destroy my ambitions. Back then, and even today, after nineteen years in the ministry, some have tried to persecute me, talking about me behind my back, choosing to recognize me only as a convict. To this day, I live with these issues on a daily basis, despite being out of prison for more than twenty years. Perhaps, in a sense, it is like what the Apostle Paul endured—but I adopted his positive perspective: "Three times I appealed to the Lord about this, that it would leave me, but he said to me, 'My grace is sufficient for you, for power is made perfect in weakness'" (2 Corinthians 12:8–9a, NRSV).

I realize there are people who would rather see me off the map if possible, but I am thankful that God is still on the throne. Several years ago, I began to realize that some people in the world can have an evil heart, but it is not true of all people. The latter are the people with whom I rise each day to share life and living. Despite the mean-spirited people who have crossed my path, God has blessed me with some very close and dear friends. There are not many, but they are enough for me, and I am happy with them being in my life.

It is apparent that I will never totally escape the demeaning name-calling, negative labels, and prejudices, both personal and racial, and the reality that some still want to bring me down because they think I have accomplished too much in life as an ex-convict. I realize those negative and mean perceptions are still present, however well masked, throughout society. But when I decided to honor my call to serve Jesus Christ, he delivered me from such people to become a witness for his glory and grace. As it says in Isaiah 53:5, "But he was wounded for our transgressions, crushed for our iniquities; upon him was the punishment that made us whole, and by his bruises we are healed."

There is a difference between being released from prison and getting out of prison. Being released from prison is when the system opens the locked gates and ends someone's confinement. Getting out of prison means removing all the things in one's mind that caused one to go or return to prison. People getting out of prison must get the causes of imprisonment out of their entire thought processes. That's how one truly gets out of prison, by getting rid of all the things from your mind that led to or could lead back to prison. To change a life, a life change must be made. Such a changed life can be accomplished in Jesus Christ if we let him. As it says in Romans 12:2, "Do not be conformed to this world, but be transformed by the renewing of your minds, so that you may discern what is the will of God—what is good and acceptable and perfect."

When we surrender ourselves to Jesus Christ and give him authority over our lives, he will give us new friends and a new family. This brings to life the passage in John 12:24, "Very truly, I tell you, unless a grain of wheat falls into the earth and dies, it remains just a single grain; but if it dies, it bears much fruit."

Today, I can say unequivocally that Jesus Christ totally changed my life! As I found out, sometimes it is necessary to reconcile with families and friends but remain as distant associates, yet without hostilities or resentments. Love trumps all and everything—we love because our Lord and Savior Jesus Christ loves us: "This is my commandment, that you love one another as I have loved you" (John 15:12).

A Complete 180-Degree Turn

> People will often forget the things you did to them, but seldom do they forget how you made them feel.[54]
>
> —Maya Angelou

54. From a Facebook post by Maya Angelou on March 15, 2014. AZ Quotes, "Maya Angelou," accessed Dec. 27, 2017, http://www.azquotes.com/author/440-Maya_Angelou.

The second time I went to prison, I thought my life was over. I was alone, and my family—except for one of my brothers who was a schoolteacher—did not want anything to do with me. This brother visited me and left money on my account so I could have food to eat, but he passed away in 1993. It was strange to me that my sister and her husband—the one who took in my siblings and me when my father passed away—subsequently began to visit. It was like they had a habit of showing up after someone died.

They came one day to tell me that my brother had passed, but only my sister returned from time to time to visit me. I thought about and hoped for a good relationship between us, but it wasn't genuine. I know that I was difficult growing up, but I always loved my siblings, even though not all of them loved me. What I later realized is that I did not become a difficult, rebellious young boy until after my sister and her husband had come into my life, especially when I was torn from my church. My mother had nine children and I was the baby of the family. I always knew who loved me and who did not. Even so, I still loved them because they were family, regardless of our history of estrangement, resentment, and distance.

I met some good people and made some good friendships in prison, including inmates, officers, and prison administrators. I became a clerk for a ranking administrator, in which position I was taught a lot about the prison business. Some of my college professors became both friends and mentors to me, and many of these people are my friends to this day. Several were instrumental in my growing up and maturing as a man and my becoming educated. God was shaping my spiritual formation, and it was God's people in prison who were there to help and encourage me. God is always good!

I wanted to make my mother and father and my siblings proud of me, but except for the brother who visited me, my siblings were not very friendly toward me. Even after I got out of prison, they remained distant and negative toward me. I believe God took me there to reveal to me the nature of my hurt and the dynamics of my failures. Indeed, those discoveries were hurtful, but Jesus Christ worked on me well and mightily enough, so that I came to the point where I loved them anyway. I tried my best to express my affections to them, but their responses informed me that they did not want to reconnect. In time, Christ nudged me that it was time to place them in his hands.

Nothing I shared with them about my goals and aspirations meant anything to them. They only wanted to remember and remind me of my past behavior. In a real sense, isn't this the problem in society at large? I believe that ex-prisoners who have changed need to prove that they are different, but there is a point where there is nothing even the most transformed ex-con can do to persuade those who will not be persuaded that change is possible.

As any human being can imagine, I was deeply hurt coming home after more than twenty years of prison to a family with such negative, hurtful, and mean remarks. I had heard that this would be the case, but I was still surprised to be received as unwholesome, unwelcome, and unaccepted as a part of the family. Regardless of their lack of compassion toward me, because I really was different, I loved them anyway. I am reminded of the Marvin Sapp song, "Never Would Have Made It," especially the line, "I'm stronger, I'm wiser, I'm better, much better."[55]

Through much soul-searching, study, prayer, and reflection, I understand myself and my life much better today. God has blessed me to learn and grow beyond measures I never thought I would ever achieve. I have lived to see the realities of the terrible visions that people warned me would happen in my life. I have also lived to see the grand visions that people spoke over my life after God had spoken to them.

In closing, it appears in too many instances that our society has become maliciously angry, with justice swung as a weapon trying to protect the fragile peace onto which we are hanging by a thread. Righteousness and goodwill toward men is on the run, and our human decency-parched democracy looks like it could use some water. Why are we, as a society, so angry, malicious, and disrespectful? Maybe, just maybe, we would do better by each other if we would seek fellowship more often with each other, turning more toward Christ, rather than turning on each other. If we could each manage to do a little more of

55. Marvin Sapp, "Never Would Have Made It," Thirsty album (RCA/Jive, 2007).

this, we would see more of Christ in each other, and as a society, we would see more of Christ in the world.

I leave you with a famous statement by Marianne Williamson, which inspired me during some of my darkest days:

> Our deepest fear is not that we are inadequate; our deepest fear is that we are powerful beyond measure. It is our light, not our darkness that most frightens us. We ask ourselves who am I to be brilliant, gorgeous, talented, fabulous? Actually, who are you *not* to be? You are a child of God. Your playing small does not serve the world. There is nothing enlightened about shrinking so that other people won't feel insecure around you. We are all meant to shine, as children do. We were born to make manifest the glory of God that is within us. It is not just in some of us; it's in everyone. And as we let our own light shine, we unconsciously give other people permission to do the same. As we're liberated from our own fear, our presence automatically liberates others.[56]

Becoming a child of God ultimately is what saved my life and gave me a life worth living. Like another famous quote by Ernest Hemingway—"The world breaks everyone, and afterward, some are strong at the broken places"[57]—legal injustice and prison broke me, but then God stepped

56. From *Return to Love* by Marianne Williamson (New York: Harper Collins, 1992), 190–91. This quote is often said to have been used in a speech by Nelson Mandela.
57. AZ Quotes, "Ernest Hemingway Quotes," accessed Dec. 28, 2017, http://www.azquotes.com/author/6539-Ernest_Hemingway.

in and intervened, bringing to life this passage from Genesis 50:20 "As for you, you meant evil against me, but God meant it for good in order to bring about this present result."

While writing this, I reflected many times over my life and the years that had brought me to that dark cell in Houston's Harris County Jail. Despite how I felt about anyone or anything that had happened in my life, ultimately, I was responsible for the unwise choices I had made in my life. But that was not the end. That district attorney laughed at me as he walked away because I would not confess to a crime I did not commit. But during the incident with the district attorney, I began to hear my grandfather's voice again, the voice that taught me just who Jesus Christ was as he read scripture to me every evening after supper. That's the day I decided I would trust Jesus Christ and listen for his voice to speak to me. When the district attorney returned to the hold-over cell I was in and asked me what I wanted to do, I said, "Do whatever you want to do; my grandfather told me about Jesus Christ. Jesus will save me." Again, he laughed. Several years passed while I was in prison and I waited. Then, finally, I heard Jesus Christ speaking to me. I was in the presence of the Lord in a prison cell. As Matthew 16:25 says, "For those who want to save their life will lose it, and those who lose their life for my sake will find it."

POSTSCRIPT

As I reflected on and prayed about ways to further enhance and improve the book while still bringing the project to a close, I decided that it would be best at some point to write another book to explore further the social justice issues that have been raised here. For now, this book broaches those subjects, provides some graphic detail from an insider's perspective, and offers some insightful solutions, but mainly it tells my story—both as an inmate of twenty years and as a pastor for even longer. Pastor Marvin is not the same man he was when he was Inmate Marvin, and telling my story includes my dramatic transformation as well as offering the reader handles on the restorative justice ministry. Most importantly, this book communicates the power of the gospel to change anyone, at any time, and in any place in life.

Within the above context, I hope the reader will give me some latitude to add a few closing thoughts regarding the social justice issues. After my release, it was the daily news reported via television and other media outlets that aroused me to action. I thought I could effectively respond to the critical issues that had begun to dominate the media outlets nationwide. I had given a great deal of thoughtfulness toward ideas that could improve and provide a better, healthier transparency between society and the criminal justice system in Texas and elsewhere. I think after serving twenty years and sixty-one days in

Texas prisons, I do have some unique input to offer that may be helpful, especially since my contribution comes through servant ministry—a focus that must dominate the discussion.

I lived through some very turbulent days and nights in one of the meanest, toughest prisons in the Texas prison system, respectfully known as the Texas Department of Corrections at the time I went into prison. I learned what the sentencing judge meant when he said, "I sentence you to ninety-nine years of 'hard labor for convicts and only convicts.'" Now, thinking about the term in retrospect, I realize the judge was specifically invoking the Thirteenth Amendment of the US Constitution when he said that. As I ponder these grim realities today, it invokes feelings of fear, disdain, and contempt that rise to the surface even after all these years. Where would such an idea—"hard labor reserved only for convicts"—come from, and why? Where, why, and how could this aspect of the original language of the Thirteenth Amendment become useful in contemporary society?

Neither slavery nor involuntary servitude, except as punishment for crime whereof the party shall have been duly convicted, shall exist within the United States, or any place subject to their jurisdiction.

—THIRTEENTH AMENDMENT TO THE US CONSTITUTION

During my imprisonment, I survived by the grace and mercy of Jesus Christ who protected me through the darkest, most difficult, most demeaning, and most inhumane time in my life. I heard death screams through the nights and I witnessed killings throughout my days in prison. I was worked exactly like a pre-Civil War slave, just as the judge had said, through "convict labor."

This term explicitly means slave labor sanctioned as legal under the US Constitution. The first day after working in the fields, I went into my cell and sat down on the floor and cried. I fell asleep on the cement floor that evening as my entire body screamed in pain. I know what it feels like and looks like to be a slave. It is the most terrible, degrading inhumanity I have ever experienced, and I lived and breathed it. It was only through the grace and mercy of Jesus Christ that I survived. Thank you, Jesus Christ, my Lord and Savior, that I'm still here!

For years on end, I performed slave labor from dawn to dusk in fields of cotton, corn, watermelon, potatoes, broom corn, and much more. The term *convict labor* is applied intentionally because it is the kind of labor that is considered inhumane and constitutionally illegal—except as outlined in the often-overlooked clause of the Thirteenth Amendment. I encourage anyone who has not read it to do so (see the sidebar).

I saw men beaten to death, stabbed to death, and raped, and some died as a show of unconcerned cold-heartedness. I know of men killed for a bag of coffee, a bag of cookies, over gambling, or for looking at or staring at someone. I saw men killed simply because someone did not care for them as a person for petty reasons. The popular saying during difficult times such as these was "Get it like you live," which simply meant that everything in prison is done the hard way. I also got into fights, some of which I came out through okay, and others of which it was just enough to say I at least stood up to the fight. On more than one occasion, I faced death, and there were times I had to fight for my life. I lived in fear for what seemed like a lifetime, but "Grace and mercy took me in," as Lee Williams's gospel song says.

I want to reiterate that it is not my intention to disparage or say negative things about the Texas prison system. Like most institutions, and life in general, change is sometimes needed even when it may be slow and painful—and TDCJ has come a very long way from the way it was when I was incarcerated. I practically grew up in prison, which isn't something I'm proud of, but I am thankful and blessed to have fully matured and become a contributing, productive citizen who is engaged in life in meaningful ways. Many of my friends did not survive their own drug abuse, criminal lifestyle, or incarceration.

Much of my ministry today—returning to prisons preaching the gospel of Jesus Christ—is propelled by their memories. Because I am blessed to still be alive, I believe that my former and passed friends would expect me to try to inspire others to come off the streets and off drugs to make sense of and better use of their lives. Because I am blessed to still be on top of the ground, and the ground is not on top of me, I hope those who have gone ahead of me can hear me, and I hope those still behind bars will listen. As Morgan Freeman said in *Shawshank Redemption*, "Get busy living or get busy dying."

I am deeply thankful that Jesus Christ would save an old crook like me and still call me his child. That's "amazing grace"! To God be the glory!

Forward Thought

There are many men and women who continue to live under extenuating mandatory sentencing parole laws that prohibit their basic human liberties by prolonged prison sentences that cannot be completed in a lifetime.

EPILOGUE

CURRENT MINISTRY

In 2017 alone, Newgate Fellowship's prison ministry went to five different TDCJ units, conducting a total of twenty services. A total of thirty volunteers ministered to nearly 3,500 inmates, with 140 coming to Christ. The following incident happened during a 2018 visit to a male prison:

Recently I was invited to come and speak to inmates incarcerated in one of TDCJ's maximum security units. These were inmates who were denouncing gang affiliation, many of whom had been gang members for as long as twenty years. I spoke to 168 men in total, divided into two different groups. I spoke to each group for an hour and a half. The first group was a racially diverse group, the presentation went well, and I was well received by the inmates.

The second group was racially composed of Caucasian and Hispanic men. This group was initially stern and resigned, and appeared to be unconcerned and detached. Some had large swastikas and other menacing tattoos. For the first fifteen or twenty minutes, everyone sat with their arms crossed, unsympathetically preoccupied. Clearly, they were unwilling to listen to anything I had to say.

Initially, I did not realize that there was not one African American inmate among this group of men. When

I recognized the racial difference after a few minutes, I was taken aback, but only momentarily. I knew that I was a Christian and a pastor in the service of Jesus Christ. Therefore, there was no idea of race, only the fellowship of men regardless of race. I was there to encourage them toward the path of righteousness and goodness. I wanted them to know that Jesus Christ loves them and was waiting to receive them, to renew and transform them into men of honor. I wanted to remind them that they could become good men with honorable families, children, and grandchildren, all of whom had been waiting for their homecoming, their affection, and their nurturing. It was time for them to get into the picture rather than asking for pictures to be sent to them.

After about twenty minutes, a couple of the men extended their fists toward each other for a fist bump, which signals approval! They smiled and began to echo words that were encouraging to me and the case managers attending the presentation. Before long, other men began to exchange fist bumps and hand slapping, with more smiles and encouraging comments for me to continue. One man stood up and slapped his chest, saying, "That's good, Marvin, that's for me!"

Other men commented, "Come on, Pastor Marvin, don't stop, bring it on!" Incredibly, their responses became thunderous, which was deeply moving for me, the case managers, and the guards. I was reminded of the

Apostle Paul and Silas in the Philippian prison in the book of Acts, chapter 16.

Afterward, the program director, case managers, and guards told me that they had never seen that kind of response from those men in seventeen years! These were inmates who had been incarcerated in administrative segregation for several years. Several of the employees attending the presentation spoke to me through teary eyes and scratchy voices as they cleared their throats.

The employees thanked me for what I had been able to do among the men. I replied that I did not do anything, that their response was the result of the ministry, work, and power of Jesus Christ. I said, "Look at God; look at Jesus Christ. All glory and honor goes to God and Jesus Christ because all grace and mercy emanates from God in Christ. I am only the vessel Christ uses, a work in his hands."

Several of the men have since expressed their desire to correspond with me and the church, and I welcome their correspondence in the fellowship of Christian believers!

BIBLIOGRAPHY

"After Prison: Roadblocks to Reentry, A Report on State Legal Barriers Facing People with Criminal Records." New York: Legal Action Center, 2004. Accessed Jan. 5, 2018, www.lac.org/roadblocks.html.

Alexander, Michelle. *The New Jim Crow in the Age of Colorblindness*. New York: The New Press, 2012.

American Civil Liberties Union. "Racial Disparities in Sentencing" (Oct. 27, 2014). Accessed Dec. 22, 2017, https://www.aclu.org/sites/default/files/assets/141027_iachr_racial_disparities_aclu_submission_0.pdf.

AZ Quotes. "Booker T. Washington Quotes." Accessed Jan. 12, 2017, http://www.azquotes.com/author/15322-Booker_T_Washington.

——. "Ernest Hemingway Quotes." Accessed Dec. 28, 2017, http://www.azquotes. com/author/6539-Ernest_Hemingway.

——. "Frederick Douglass Quotes." Accessed Dec. 24, 2017, http://www.azquotes.com/author/4104-Frederick_Douglass.

——. "George MacDonald Quotes." Accessed Dec. 24, 2017, http://www.azquotes.com/author/9199-George_MacDonald.

——. "Maya Angelou Quotes." Accessed Dec. 27, 2017, http://www.azquotes.com/author/440-Maya_Angelou.

——. "Ravi Zacharias." Accessed Jan. 5, 2018, http://www.azquotes.com/quotes/topics/faith.html.

——. "Victor Hugo Quotes about Education." Accessed Dec. 24, 2017, http://www.azquotes.com/author/7021-Victor_Hugo/tag/education.

Blakinger, Keri. "Texas Prisons Eliminate Use of Solitary Confinement for Punitive Reasons." *Houston Chronicle* (Sept. 21, 2017). Accessed Dec. 21, 2017, http://www.houstonchronicle.com/news/houston-texas/houston/article/Texas-prisons-eliminate-use-of-solitary-12219437.php.

Diagnostic and Statistical Manual of Mental Disorders: DSM-IV, 4th ed. Washington, D.C.: American Psychiatric Association, 1994.

Dictionary.com. "Hypervigilance." Accessed Feb. 12, 2011, http://dictionary.reference.com/browse/hypervigilance.

Dyer, Joel. *The Perpetual Prisoner Machine: How America Profits from Crime*. Boulder, CO: Westview Press, 2000.

Frederick Douglass, Philip Sheldon Foner, and Yuval Taylor. *Frederick Douglass: Selected Speeches and Writings*. Chicago: Chicago Review Press, 1999.

——. *The Essential Douglass: Selected Writings and Speeches*. Indianapolis: Hackett Publishing, 2016.

Good Reads. "Mahatma Ghandi Quotes." Accessed Jan. 13, 2017, https://www.goodreads.com/quotes/22155-i-like-your-christ-i-do-not-like-your-christians.

Hanson, Kathryn, and Deborah Stipek. "Schools v. Prisons: Education's the Way to Cut Prison Population" (May 16, 2014). Accessed Dec. 22, 2017, https://ed.stanford.edu/in-the-media/schools-v-prisons-educations-way-cut-prison-population-op-ed-deborah-stipek.

Hawkins, Steven. "Education vs. Incarceration" (Dec. 6, 2010). Accessed Dec. 22, 2017, http://prospect.org/article/education-vs-incarceration.

Hrebik, Kevin. "Within the Context of Physical Scars, Applying Scripture and Bowen Theory to Help Inmates Understand and Overcome Their Emotional Scars." Doctor of Ministry dissertation. Houston Graduate School of Theology, 2012.

Lee College. "About Lee College Huntsville Center." Accessed Jan. 13, 2017, http://www.lee.edu/lchc/about-lchc/.

McArthur, Judith N., and Harold J. Smith. *Minnie Fisher Cunningham: A Suffragists's Life in Politics*. New York: Oxford University Press, 2003.

National Park Service. "Frederick Douglass." Accessed Dec. 24, 2017, https://www.nps.gov/frdo/learn/historyculture/frederickdouglass.htm. The Frederick Douglass National Historic Site is in Washington, DC.

Pedersen, Daniel, Daniel Shapiro, and Ann McDaniel. *Newsweek* 108, no. 14 (Oct. 6, 1986): 46–61.

Perkinson, Robert. *Texas Tough: Inside America's Prison Empire*. New York: Henry Holt and Company, 2010.

Ragland, James. "If Texas' Prison Population Were a City, it Would Be the State's 20th Largest." *Dallas News* (Sept 2016). Accessed Jan. 15, 2018, https://www.dallasnews.com/opinion/commentary/2016/09/16/texas-prison-population-city-states-20th-largest.

Texas Criminal Justice Coalition. "Parole and Reentry." Accessed Dec. 21, 2017, https://www.texascjc.org/parole-reentry.

Texas Department of Criminal Justice. *Criminal Justice Connections* 24, no. 3 (Jan/Feb 2017). Accessed Dec. 21, 2017, https://www.tdcj.state.tx.us/connections/JanFeb2017/Images/JanFeb2017_agency_lbb.pdf.

Texas Department of Criminal Justice Statistical Report (FY 2016). Accessed Jan. 15, 2018, https://www.tdcj.state.tx.us/documents/Statistical_Report_FY2016.pdf.

Tozer, A. W. *The Root of the Righteous*. Chicago: Moody Publishers, 2015.

Wikipedia. "Ruiz v. Estelle." Accessed Dec. 19, 2017, https://en.wikipedia.org/wiki/Ruiz_v._Estelle.

Williamson, Marianne. *Return to Love*. New York: Harper Collins, 1992.

BIBLE SOURCES

ABOUT THE AUTHOR

Marvin Hood is a pastor for the United Methodist Church and volunteers with the Texas Department of Criminal Justice to preach to inmates and help them get their lives back on track. Having been incarcerated himself for twenty years, he is well aware of the challenges inmates face both in prison and after they are released. His mission is to serve men, women, and families impacted as a result of crime and incarceration.

Pastor Marvin received two associate's degrees and a bachelor's degree while still in prison, he graduated from Perkins School of Theology after his release, and is a certified pastoral care specialist. In his free time, he enjoys studying, peeking into philosophy, and helping others. His hobbies include landscaping and playing pool. Pastor Marvin lives in Cypress, Texas, with his wife Bonita.

To learn more, visit newgateumc.com